John Starkie Gardner

Armour in England

From the earliest times to the Seventeenth century

John Starkie Gardner

Armour in England

From the earliest times to the Seventeenth century

ISBN/EAN: 9783741178450

Manufactured in Europe, USA, Canada, Australia, Japa

Cover: Foto ©Andreas Hilbeck / pixelio.de

Manufactured and distributed by brebook publishing software (www.brebook.com)

John Starkie Gardner

Armour in England

ARMOUR IN ENGLAND

FROM THE EARLIEST TIMES
TO THE SEVENTEENTH CENTURY

By

J. STARKIE GARDNER

*With Sixteen Coloured Plates
and more than Eighty other Illustrations*

LONDON
SEELEY AND CO. LIMITED, 38 GREAT RUSSELL STREET
NEW YORK: THE MACMILLAN COMPANY
1898

PART I

*ARMOUR MADE IN ENGLAND
OR FOR ENGLISHMEN*

LIST OF ILLUSTRATIONS

COLOURED PLATES

PAGE

I. Full suit of armour of Henry, Prince of Wales, in the Guard-chamber at Windsor Castle. Attributed to William Pickering, master-armourer *Frontispiece*

II. Second suit of Sir Henry Lee, Master of the Armoury, reduced facsimile of No. 19 in the Armourers' Album in the South Kensington Museum . 28

III. First suit of Sir Christopher Hatton, Captain of the Guard, and subsequently Lord Chancellor. Reduced facsimile of No. 15 in the Armourers' Album in the South Kensington Museum 40

IV. Grand-guard of the suit of George, Earl of Cumberland, in the possession of Lord Hothfield. This is a part of the 20th suit in the Armourers' Album in the South Kensington Museum 46

V. Grand-guard, used for tilting, belonging to the suit of Robert Dudley, Earl of Leicester, with the gilding restored. In the Tower of London . . 58

VI. Profile of the helmet belonging to the French suit (Fig. 32). In the Guard-chamber of Windsor Castle 76

VII. Ornament on the tapul of the breastplate belonging to the half-suit of the Earl of Essex (Fig. 35), with the original gilding slightly restored. In the Guard-chamber of Windsor Castle 90

VIII. The sword of Charles I. when Prince of Wales, 1616. The hilt entirely covered with raised gold damascened work on blue steel matrix, except the grip of silver wire work. Preserved in Windsor Castle 96

ILLUSTRATIONS IN THE TEXT

1. Hauberk, or byrnie, of chain-mail, of the fourth or fifth century, found at Vimose 11
2. Norman knights in mail hauberks and conical helmets 13
3. A complete suit of mail, with coif and mufflers ; A thirteenth-century suit, with reinforcing plates 17
4. Mail coif, flat-topped, with leather thong . 19
5. Mail coif, round-topped, with jewelled fillet . 19
6. Mail coif, conical top, with coronet and mantelet 19
7. Helmet of bronze and iron, from County Down 21

/ LIST OF ILLUSTRATIONS

	PAGE
8. Illustration of the development of plate-armour	23
9. The sleeping guards, from the Easter Sepulchre in Lincoln Cathedral	25
10. Mêlée. From MS. of the fourteenth century	29
11. The helm and crest of the Black Prince, with his shield, from his monument in Canterbury Cathedral	31
12. The helm of Richard Pembridge, K.G., from Hereford Cathedral	32
13. Bassinet from the tomb of Sir John de Melsa, Aldborough Church, Holderness	32
14. A bassinet transformed into a sallad in the fifteenth century	33
15. A ridged bassinet with banded camail; Combed and jewelled bassinet	35
16. Effigy of the Black Prince on his tomb in Canterbury Cathedral	37
17. Gauntlet from the effigy of Ralph Neville, Earl of Westmoreland, in Staindrop Church, Durham; Gauntlet from the effigy of Sir Thomas Cawne, Ightham Church, Kent	41
18. Helm from the tomb of Henry V. in Westminster Abbey	48
19. Effigy of Richard Beauchamp, Earl of Warwick, on his tomb in St. Mary's Church, Warwick	53
20. The Earl of Warwick slays a "mighty Duke." From the Beauchamp MS.	55
21. The Duke of Gloucester and Earls of Warwick and Stafford chase the Duke of Burgundy from the walls of Calais. From the Beauchamp MS.	57
22. Sallad in St. Mary's Hall, Coventry; Helm of Sir Giles Capel	59
23. English tournament helm over the tomb of John Beaufort, Duke of Somerset, in Wimborne Minster	60
24. Helm of Sir John Gostwick, in Willington Church	61
25. The entry of Queen Isabel into Paris in 1390. From MS. of Froissart	63
26. Armet of Sir George Brooke, K.G., 8th Lord Cobham	65
27. English armet from the collection of Seymour Lucas, A.R.A.	65
28. Complete suit for fighting on foot, made for Henry VIII.	67
29. Suit made for Henry VIII. by Conrad Seusenhofer of Innsbrück, 1511-1514	71
30. Part of a suit made for Sir Christopher Hatton	79
31. Armour of Robert Dudley, Earl of Leicester, 1566-1588	83
32. A suit of French armour, early seventeenth century	87
33. Italian suit of blued and gilded steel covered with appliqués of gold	89
34. A part of the ornament of the Italian suit (Fig. 33), drawn real size	91
35. Demi-suit of the Earl of Essex, with closed helmet, magnificently engraved and gilt	93
36. Sword, probably of James I., with basket hilt, entirely covered with raised gold damascening	95
37. The sword of John Hampden, with hilt of carved steel	97

PLATE I.—Full suit of armour of Henry, Prince of Wales, in the guard-chamber at Windsor Castle. Attributed to William Pickering, master armourer.

ARMOUR IN ENGLAND

I

The Britons—An Early Age of Plate-Armour

It is the nature of islands to exhibit some peculiarities in their fauna and flora, and this insularity is no less pronounced in the manners and customs of the human beings inhabiting them. Thus even the stone implements of Britain of remote prehistoric days can readily be distinguished by the expert ; and we have the authority of Sir John Evans for regarding our types of bronze celts and weapons as both peculiar and indigenous. On first taking a place in history several strange and extra-European customs were noticed in these isles by Cæsar, such as the use of chariots in war, and dyeing the skin blue with woad : British nations were, moreover, frequently ruled by queens, and some practised the rare and difficult, and very far from barbaric, art of enamelling on bronze.

Modern opinion is at present opposed to the theory that the culture and civilisation of Western Europe originated exclusively in the East, and is inclined to regard our primitive arts and crafts as indigenous. That this must in a large measure be true appears sufficiently established ; but the large and excellently-made bronze bucklers with concentric rings of bosses or studs, called the clypeus, the singular art of enamelling, the use of studs of coral for embellishing weapons and trinkets, the chariots of war and the government by women, all so remote from savagery, and so intimately connected with Eastern civilisation, compel the belief that these isles did actually at some distant time possess a privileged and intimate communication with the East. The old and rooted tradition of a direct traffic in tin between Britain and Phœnicia cannot yet in fact be safely abandoned.

These arts and practices, however, only fall within the scope of our subject so far as they were applied to arms and weapons. One of these, very rarely used for the embellishment of arms in later times, is that of enamelling, a process unknown to the Romans. Philostratus, who wrote in the third century, referring to some coloured horse-trappings, observed, " They say that the Barbarians who live in the Ocean pour these colours on to heated bronze, and that they adhere, become hard as stone, and preserve the designs which are made in them." The bronze to be enamelled was cast with the pattern upon it, and the colours used were varied and bright, but opaque. Some brilliant horse-trappings with purely Celtic decorations and a few sword-hilts are known, but the bulk of cast bronze enamelled ware consisted of brooches, seal-boxes, cups, and vases, all Romano-British in design. A much rarer enamel is found on beaten or repoussé bronze armour. Pliny, in the Natural History, remarks that the Gauls were in the habit of adorning their swords, shields, and helmets with coral, but an immense demand springing up in India, it became unprocurable. We find accordingly that resort was had in England to enamel to reproduce the effect of the coral studs. In the British Museum is an oblong shield of Celtic design, found in the Witham, embellished with coral, but a smaller and handsomer shield beside it, found in the Thames, has gold cloisonné studs of blood-red enamel. The curious Celtic reproduction of the Roman peaked helmet, and the horned helmet found in the Thames, both from the Meyrick collection, are also decorated with small raised bosses cross-hatched to retain red enamel, some of which still adheres. The horned brazen helmet should, according to Diodorus Siculus, be a relic of, or borrowed from, the Belgic Gauls, who inhabited so much of this part of England. The gem-like effect of the enamelled studs, like single drops of red on the golden bronze, must have been most refined; it is altogether too restrained to have originated with the enameller, who usually covers his surfaces. The identity of workmanship of these arms with the Irish bronze and enamel work suggests that some of those who produced them passed over and found with their traditions and arts a peaceful refuge in the sister isle.

Tacitus, however, states most explicitly that the Britons wore neither helmets nor armour, and were not able, therefore, under Caractacus, to maintain their resistance. Herodianus also, relating the expedition of Severus 250 years after Cæsar's invasion, presents an extraordinary picture of savagery. He observes that the Britons were a most warlike and sanguinary race, carrying only a small shield and a spear, and a sword girded to their naked bodies. "Of a breastplate or helmet they knew not the use, esteeming them an impediment through the marshes." They encircled their necks and loins with iron rings as an evidence of wealth, instead of gold, and went naked rather than conceal the tattoos of different animals which covered and gave a blue cast to their bodies.

In striking contrast to this picture are the large number of chariots employed in war and the extraordinary skill displayed in handling them. Cæsar states that Cassivelaunus, when totally defeated and a fugitive, was still accompanied by 4000 charioteers; the basis probably of Pomponius Mela's later statement that 4000 two-horsed chariots armed with scythes formed part of that chieftain's army. Having proved ineffectual against Roman discipline, this arm was perhaps soon abandoned, since we find little further mention of war-chariots, though cavalry did not cease to form part of a British army. In process of time the subjugated Britons must have become completely Romanised as to arms, and accustomed to wear the helmet, greaves, and corselet, either of one piece or formed of smaller and more flexible plates or scales. Though the manhood of the country enrolled in disciplined cohorts and legions had deserted it, Roman weapons must have been the arms of those who remained when the Romans finally retired from Britain in 410.

In the two succeeding centuries, which were to elapse before the country definitely inclined to become English, an intensely Celtic feeling, embodied in the legends of King Arthur and wholly opposed to Roman ideas, had time to spring up. Judged by their ornament, it is to this period that most of the bronze enamelled arms and trappings in the British Museum belong. The golden corselet found in a barrow in Flint, together with many traditions of the finding of golden armour, such as the helmet of pure gold set with gems found in a bronze vase and presented to Katharine of Arragon, suggest the idea that serviceable qualities became sacrificed to a love of display. At this time it is said the Britons, in obsolete and fantastic panoply, bore an evil reputation, as being vain and fruitful in menaces, but slow and little to be feared in action. Their frightfully demoralised state, if not greatly overdrawn by Gildas, called for a day of reckoning and the condign, almost exterminating, punishment which overtook them. The agents destined to execute the vengeance of Providence were the Frisian pirates, the scourge of the Channel, who had with difficulty been kept in awe by the most powerful Roman fleets. The country, left to the divided rule of clergy, nobles, and municipalities, and described as "glittering with the multitude of cities built by the Romans," presented a tempting and easy prey to these professors of rapine. They were Teutons, who relied mainly on the Fram or spear-like javelin, as when Tacitus described them, and still carried the round gaudily-painted buckler, though then strengthened with an iron umbo and rim. Their weapons had been perfected in a long series of grim experiences in actual war, and they had added to their equipment a sword and dagger, and some kind of simple headpiece. That they had adopted any complete defence of plate-armour in the Roman fashion is improbable, but they were apparently entirely unacquainted with chain-mail. In the history of armour in Britain this period, taken as a whole, can only be regarded as a very primitive age of plate. To be an efficient protection plate-armour must, however, be of an intolerable weight, at least to men on foot, making celerity of movement impossible. We cannot close the chapter better than by instancing the dreadful fate of the Æduan Crupellarians, related by Tacitus, who clothed themselves in unwieldy iron plate, impenetrable to sword and javelin. Though the main army was overthrown, these kept their ranks as if rooted to the ground, until, fallen upon with hatchets and pickaxes, armour and men were crushed together and left on the ground an inanimate mass. This lesson was not forgotten by the nations of Europe who fought on foot with Rome, and no such use of body-armour among them is again recorded.

II

The Mailed Warrior

THE appearance of the mail-clad warrior opens up an entirely new era in the history of European armour. The light plate defences worn by the Mediterranean nations, whether Greeks, Etruscans, or Romans, were never calculated to secure immunity from wounds; and as a fighting equipment they went down before mail, as stone before bronze, or bronze before iron. Chain-mail body-armour is distinctly represented on the Trajan column, and wherever worn, whether by the Scythian, the Parthian who was armoured down to his horse's hoofs, or the dreaded Sassanian horse, it seems to have flashed like a beacon of victory, and its wearers ever appear in history as Rome's most dreaded and formidable foes.

The Scandinavian also, isolated so long and unknown in history, suddenly burst upon Europe as a new and even more redoubtable mail-clad warrior. How so remote a people became acquainted with chain-mail can only be surmised, but it was perhaps through some Scythian channel not open to Western Europe. That the ravaging Viking landed on our shores equipped in mail, the "war nets" of Beowulf, "woven by the smiths, hand-locked, and riveted"; "shining over the waters" or in "the ranks of battle," is sufficiently recorded by the Chroniclers. Shirts of mail, called "byrnies," attributed to even the fourth and fifth centuries, are found in Danish peat-bogs fashioned of rings welded and riveted in alternate rows as neatly and skilfully as can possibly be, and all made by the hammer, if it be a fact that wire-drawing was not invented till nearly a thousand years later. The almost perfect specimen we figure, one-tenth the natural size, was found at Vimose, with portions of others. Some have also been found at Thorsberg, and in a burial-place of Roman age in Jutland.

Besides the mail defence, the Danes were armed with a shield, an iron cap, lance, axe, and sword. Thus equipped they proved for a long time almost irresistible, and ventured on the most dangerous and desperate undertakings. When we reflect on their adventurous voyages, the reckless attacks on powerful nations made by mere handfuls of men, and the gallant pertinacity they at all times displayed, it is impossible not to admire their exalted courage. It is easy to detect a rugged poetry, almost chivalry of a kind, underlying the Viking nature, in spite of ruthless cruelty, while the exaltation of deceit when practised on an enemy into a virtue is but a germ of modern statecraft. Their lives depending at every moment on the quality of their weapons caused these to be invested, particularly the sword, with a mystic glamour, which scarcely died out with chivalry itself, and lingers even yet in the more important functions of state. The chieftain's sword was in fact his inseparable companion, known and endeared to his followers by a name symbolic of the havoc they had seen it wreak upon the enemy, and its fame in sagas was as undying as its owner's. Tradition elevated the maker of the sword of Odin, a smith, we must believe, who forged swords of uncommon excellence, into a demigod; and has handed down the story of how he made a blade called Mimung so keenly tempered that when challenged to try conclusions with one Amilias, a rival, it sliced him so cleanly in two as he sat in his armour, that the cut only became apparent when, as he rose to shake himself, he fell dead in two halves. The name of this prince of craftsmen yet lives in the mysterious Wayland Smith of English folk-lore. Another vaunting smith Mimer was slain by the sword Grauer wielded by Sigurd; and the sword Hrunting is made famous by its owner Beowulf, the father of English lyrics. A Danish sword in the British Museum is inscribed in runes Ægenkœra, the awe-inspirer. From the Danes the exaltation of the sword passed to the English, and we find Ethelwulf, Alfred, and Athelstan bequeathing their swords by will as most precious possessions, equivalent to a brother's or sister's portion. Thence it passed, in legend at least, to the Britons, King Arthur's sword Calibon, or Excalibur, presented ultimately by Richard I. to Tancred when in Sicily, being almost as famous as Arthur himself.

Even Cæsar is provided by history with a sword named "Crocea mors," captured from him in combat by our valiant countryman Nennius. The hilts of the Danish swords are described in the *Edda* as of gold, and Beowulf speaks of hilts that were treasures of gold and jewels. Canute's

Fig. 1.—*Hauberk, or byrnie, of chain-mail, of the fourth or fifth century, found at Vimose, one-tenth of the real size; and part of another, full size, from Thorsberg. From "Danish Arts," published for the Science and Art Department.*

huiscarles and Earl Godwin's crew had swords inlaid with the precious metals, and some English swords were valued at eighty mancuses of gold.

The origin of the remarkable veneration for arms and armour, so apparent in the history of chivalry, is thus traced to wearers of mail, the first figures also to appear in something like what we regard as knightly equipment. The dress of Magnus Barefoot, described in 1093, differed probably but little from that of his predecessors, and consisted of helmet, a red shield with a golden lion, his sword called Leg-biter, a battle-axe, and a coat-of-mail, over which he wore a red silk tunic with a yellow lion.

The wearing of armour, particularly mail, on land, necessitated riding, and the northern rovers, finding the weight intolerable on their inland forays, took to horse whenever possible, harrying by this means an extent of country otherwise almost inaccessible. They even learnt in time to transport their horses over the sea, and in the ninth and tenth centuries landed in England from France as a mounted force, as their descendants after them did at Hastings. The English, on the other hand, rarely wore mail, though the spoils of the Danes might have furnished a fair supply, and they only used cavalry as a small force for scouting. An English king of the eighth century is, however, represented in mail by Strutt, and Harold and his immediate companions may have worn mail at Hastings, as represented in the Bayeux tapestry, and as he certainly did when assisting William in his war against Conan of Brittany. Handsome presents of Norman arms and armour were then made to him by Duke William. A little later we have the curious testimony of Anna Comnena, 1083-1146, that this mail, made entirely of steel rings riveted together, was wholly unknown in Byzantium, and only worn by the inhabitants of Northern Europe.

The definite conversion of the Northmen from sea-rovers to mounted men-at-arms when they settled in Normandy enabled them to lengthen their coats-of-mail, as well as their shields, lances, and swords, and to adopt many French manners and customs. But in facing the infantry wedge at Hastings, the time-honoured fighting formation of Teutonic stocks from the days of Tacitus, they did not disdain to fall back on the old Viking tactics of a pretended flight and rally, practised already by them during two centuries of warfare in England. That the English should have allowed their impenetrable ranks to be broken by so threadbare a stratagem is indeed extraordinary.

The Norman Conquest introduced into England a permanent mailclad cavalry as the chief strength of the battle, as in France, and infantry was discredited until the disputes of the sons of the Conqueror led once more to an English infantry force taking the field. The mail coat of the cavalry had in the meantime been further lengthened, and changed into a complete sheathing of steel by the addition of long sleeves and mufflers falling over the hands; leggings covering the thighs, shins, and feet; and a capuchin-like hood only leaving the eyes and nose exposed, but which could be thrown back. Thus enveloped, with a

Fig. 2.—*Norman knights in mail hauberks and conical helmets. From the Bayeux Tapestry.*

thickly-padded garment under the mail, a conical or flat-topped steel helmet, a large kite-shaped shield, and long-reaching weapons, he had little to fear when opposed to light-armed cavalry or infantry. The mail and helmets were always kept bright, as we know, but Anna Comnena adds that even the shields of steel and brass were so brightly polished as to dazzle beholders. Combined with the pennons and banners of various forms, with their glittering emblazonry, the massed men-at-arms of that day must have presented a magnificent spectacle, as the Chroniclers so frequently remind us. The coat-of-mail remained with but trifling variations the chief knightly defence until the close of the thirteenth century, and the protection it afforded was so complete that of 900 combatants who once entered battle in steel armour but three were slain. At Joppa in 1192, during a battle lasting from the rising to the setting sun, only three were killed on the side of the Crusaders ; at the battle of Lincoln only three, at Evesham (1260) one knight and two esquires, at Falkirk (1295) but one knight and thirty foot on the winning side. These somewhat random examples seem fairly to represent the loss on the side of the victors, though terrible massacres overtook the losers. The protection was such that Saladin's bravest warriors reported our men to be impenetrable; blows, they said, fell as if on rocks of flint, for our people were of iron and would yield to no blows. But though so terrible on horseback, the mailed knight, as observed by Anna Comnena, was little dangerous when dismounted. Neither had the English failed to observe this, and thus directed all their efforts to dismount the enemy. They had been severely galled by the bow at Hastings, and they came to recognise it as the one weapon likely to render them really formidable to their Norman oppressors. Henry I. encouraged its use, and we soon find the English arrows described as falling in battle like a shower on the grass or as falling snow. In a skirmish at Bourgthéroude in 1124, the first discharge brought forty horses to the ground before a stroke was struck, and eighty men-at-arms soon fell prisoners into the victors' hands. At the battle of the Standard, the cloud of arrows pierced the unarmoured Scots, and chiefly contributed to the dreadful slaughter, set down at 11,000. The effects of missile weapons were such that the mailed period of which we are speaking saw three English kings fall victims to the bow, while a fourth, Edward I., escaped a like fate by a miracle. The accounts handed down of the extraordinary range and precision attained soon afterwards by this weapon appear wholly incredible in the light of modern toxophilite displays.

The cross-bow was an even more powerful weapon, whose use had been forbidden in war, but allowed by the Pope to the Crusaders in 1139. Richard I. appears to have introduced it into the English army, which became so expert in its use that in some of the sieges conducted during the twelfth and thirteenth centuries the enemies' walls could not be manned. It is related of Richard, both at the sieges of Acre and Nottingham, that he himself slew men with this weapon. The numbers of cross-bowmen in our armies appear, however, to have been always relatively small. King John, with 400 knights, had but 250 cross-bowmen, used as skirmishers, keeping a mile in front of the army. The splendid army of Edward I. assembled at Poitou (1242), numbering 1600 knights and 20,000 foot, comprised but 700. The battle of Lincoln, however, was gained by them owing to their shot mowing down the horses of the barons, who were rendered helpless when dismounted. The cross-bow was at first bent by the hand and foot, but was afterwards of steel, when it required mechanical aids to charge it. The short and heavy bolts, called quarrels, struck with greater force than arrows, and the knight hit full on the head or breast by one was fortunate if only stunned. Instances are recorded of twofold mail and the quilted coat being penetrated by them. Cross-bowmen for a long time formed corps d'élite, the weight of the weapon and the armour causing them to be frequently mounted, and so early as King John the mounted "balistarii" were provided with one, two, or even three horses each, with carts to carry the quarrels and even the cross-bows as well. Notwithstanding superior accuracy in aim and penetrating power, it fell into disuse in England soon after the close of the thirteenth century, owing to its heavy weight and liability to damage by wet, and above all, on account of the greater rapidity with which arrows could be discharged from the long-bow,—in a ratio of something like ten to one.

Nothing is more constantly met with in chronicles than accounts of the destructive effects of missiles, whether from bow or cross-bow, upon the horses of mounted combatants; yet, apart from the poetic fancy of Wace, who mounts Fitz-Osbert on an iron-clad steed at Hastings, the first mention of horse-armour at all connected with English history is at the battle of Gisors in 1198, when Richard I. speaks of the capture of 140 sets in terms which plainly show that he then met with it for the first time. It has, however, been concluded, from the absence of any mention of horse-armour in English statutes until 1298, that it was unknown here till the close of the thirteenth century. At this time a man-at-arms in France received half as much again in pay if his horse was armoured, and in 1303 every man with an estate of 500 livres was bound to provide horse-armour. A mailed horse appears in the effigy of Sir Robert de Shirland in Sheppey, and a fine figure of a steed completely clad in mail is among the figures of *The Painted Chamber*, published by the Society of Antiquaries.

The English custom of fighting on foot, it is almost needless to add, had been adopted by the Danish and even the Norman settlers here, and during the civil wars of Henry I., Stephen, and Henry II., the leaders on both sides, including the kings in person, fought their battles dismounted, rendering horse-armour of relatively small importance.

A permanent force was raised by a law of Henry II. in 1181, compelling every burgess or freeman to possess an iron headpiece, a lance, and either a mail hauberk or a gambeson, according to his means: and this was supplemented by the addition, under Henry III. in 1253, of swords and knives to the infantry equipment, and the calling up of a reserve of those possessed of less than 40s. of land, armed with scythes, long-handled axes, knives, and other rustic weapons. Soon afterwards a wild Welsh and Cornish infantry was enrolled, and we hear of lagers and intrenchments, and in 1302 one of the first really crushing defeats is inflicted on chivalry at the hands of burghers by the men of Bruges, who slew forty counts and barons at Cambray.

This extensive arming of the population led to the formation of bands of outlaws, who devastated the country, something in the manner of the free-companies of France at a later time. A young man named William, declining to acknowledge Lewis of France in 1216, drew together a thousand bowmen and conducted a guerilla warfare in the forests of Sussex. The still more renowned Adam Gordon infested the woody country between Wilts and Hants until Prince Edward at last, about 1267, overcame him in single combat. The ancient Ballads abound with instances of such exploits, which are embodied in the romance of Robin Hood.

A contemporary of Richard I. describes the equipment of an English foot-soldier as consisting of an iron headpiece, a coif and coat-of-mail, and "a tissue of many folds of linen, difficult of penetration and artificially worked with the needle, vulgarly called a pourpoint." He was taught to receive cavalry with the right knee on the ground, the left leg bent, the shield in the left hand and the butt of the lance in the ground with the point to the enemy. Between every two lances was a cross-bowman with a rear rank to load while the front shot. Against this formation the Moslem cavalry's "surging charges foamed themselves away," and as at Waterloo, the retreating squadrons were charged again and again by our heavy-armed horse. On the other hand, the same tactics, when employed against forces largely composed of English archers, were

FIG. 3.

1. A complete suit of mail, with coif and mufflers, late twelfth century, said to have been found in a coffin in Goring Church.
2. A thirteenth-century suit, with reinforcing plates, said to have been found with the other.

unsuccessful; thus the Welsh in 1295 set their long spears on the ground with points towards the cavalry, but the Earl of Warwick placed an archer between every two horsemen and routed them. Wallace's massed pikemen, three years later, were broken by Edward's archers and military engines, and routed by the men-at-arms, who dashed into the openings.

It does not appear that any special study of mail has been undertaken, or that any good collection of mail has been formed, nor have the many varieties been arranged chronologically in the order in which they appeared. Materials for such a study exist, though not very abundantly, in the Tower, the British Museum, the collection at Woolwich and Dover Castle, the Armourers' Hall, Warwick Castle, Parham, and in other private collections, and from these and the effigies of mailed knights it can be seen that an almost endless variety exists, not only in the sizes of the links, which vary from $\frac{1}{8}$ to $\frac{3}{4}$ of an inch in diameter, but in the sections of the wire used, which may be round, flat, triangular, trapeziform, quadrate, polygonal, etc. Nor is there less diversity in the method of closing the rings, which was accomplished either by welding, single or double riveting, with a flattening and more or less overlapping of the links, soldering or merely butting. Again, there are many ways of arranging the links, producing mail of very different weights, either double or single, as well as mail in which certain parts are stronger than the rest. In European mail four links are usually made to pass through a centre one, though this is not an invariable rule. The statement in Beckman's *History of Inventions*, that wire-drawing was invented in the fourteenth century, was held for a long time to furnish a safe date, but two Corporations of wire-drawers occur in Etienne Boileau's *Paris Livres des Mestiers*, in the middle of the thirteenth century, and the art is actually of unknown antiquity. The mail, we read, was kept bright by barreling, but does not appear to have presented much scope for decoration. The *Edda* speaks of a byrnie of gold, and there are other allusions to gilded mail, and we find hauberks scalloped at the extremities, and finished off with rings of brass.

Two suits of mail (see Fig. 3), illustrated in the catalogue of the loan collection of Ironmongers' Hall in 1861, now in the possession of Mr. J. E. Gardner, F.S.A., are formed of unriveted links, the ends of the rings being merely butted. Their authenticity has therefore been questioned. The description of them printed in 1861 was to the effect that they had been found in a chest or in a vault of a church in Oxfordshire. In the manuscript catalogue of the collection at Parham is a note to the effect that they were found in stone coffins built in the wall of the church at Goring, Berks, supposed to be coffins of the Beche or

De Beche family, and contained skeletons, a third suit having been destroyed except the hood, which is now at Parham. However this may be, the larger suit affords a good representation of the mailed figure of the end of the twelfth, and the small one of that of the thirteenth century, with reinforcing pieces of plate. The possibility of their having been made for lying in state or funerals deserves perhaps a passing note, especially in view of their respective dimensions; and it is in any case very questionable whether the prices paid for them would have remunerated the labour of producing forgeries. Another hauberk of large size was found in Phœnix Park, Dublin, thirty years ago, but a silver badge of an O'Neil found with it showed it to have been buried not

FIG. 4.—*Mail coif, flat-topped, with leather thong.*
From the effigy of William Longespée, son of Henry II. by Fair Rosamond, who died 1227. Salisbury Cathedral.

FIG. 5.—*Mail coif, round-topped, with jewelled fillet.*
From the effigy of Robert de Vere, Earl of Oxford, died 1221. Hatfield Broad-Oak Church.

FIG. 6.—*Mail coif, conical top, with coronet and mantelet.*
From the effigy of John of Eltham, Earl of Cornwall, died 1334. Westminster Abbey.

earlier than the middle of the fifteenth century. In the thirteenth century the curious and well-known banded mail appears on effigies and other representations, which Mr. J. G. Waller, F.S.A., regards as caused by the passing of a leather thong through each alternate row of rings, for the sake of extra strength. This variety may have originated with the single thong passed through the links of the coif over the forehead and below the knee, seen in early effigies like that of William Longespée (Fig. 4) at Salisbury.

The defence of the body was for a time wholly left to the mail with the underlying gambeson, and the shield, but the head had always received the additional protection of a cap of steel, called the chapelle-de-fer, worn indifferently under or over the coif of mail. Effigies of the first half of the thirteenth century show it both round and flat at the top (Figs. 4, 5, 6, and 7). The nasal piece associated with the conical helm (Fig. 2) of the eleventh century tended to disappear in the twelfth.

The fact that English armies under Richard I. were made to abandon their ancient formation and to engage on horseback, and to rely on the battle-axe and mace as their chief weapons, and the presence of the large bodies of archers and arbalisters which he brought into the field, led to the introduction, probably by Richard himself, of the great heaume worn over the steel cap and padding, and only put on at the moment of battle. It is first seen on Richard's second seal, and consisted of a cylinder, usually flat-topped, with two horizontal clefts for vision, and strengthened by bands crossing each other over the face and top. Breathing-holes were added towards the middle of the century, and the grated front was introduced soon after, to admit more air. This is seen in the first seal of Henry III., and another advance, the movable vantail, hinged at the side, in his second seal. An oft-described specimen in the Tower weighs 13 lb. 8 oz., but is regarded by Lord Dillon, the present Curator of the Armouries, as a forgery. About 1270 we sometimes find it with a round top, though the flat top did not go quite out till the beginning of the fourteenth century. The attempts made to seize and drag it off, so often noticed by Chroniclers, led to its being secured by a chain. The further changes seen were improvements in the visor, giving better vision and more air, fixing it more securely, and so transferring the weight from the head to the shoulders, and changing the flat top to a cone, on which blows fell with less stunning effect.

These heaumes, by concealing the face, intensified a difficulty already felt at Hastings, when Duke William was obliged to raise his helmet to contradict a rumour of his death. Recognition, now become impossible, led to the use of heraldic badges, at first painted on the helm, as they already were on the shield; and of crests, first in the fan or peacock's feather shape, as on the second seal of Richard I., and afterwards to more distinctive crests and badges. The Crusading Chroniclers relate that the crests were brilliant with jewels, and they are represented as circled by coronets in the seals of Henry III. and his son Edward. The heaume of

St. Louis, 1249, was gilded. Richard himself, in gala dress, on the day after his marriage with Berengaria, is described by Vinsauf as wearing a Damascus sword with gold hilt and silver-scaled scabbard, his saddle inlaid with precious stones, his horse bitted with gold, and in place of the high defensive plates before and behind in general use two little golden lions with raised paws.

Fig. 7.—*Helmet of bronze and iron, from County Down. Twelfth century.*

Next to the headpiece the most urgent necessity was to protect the breast against the direct shock of the lance, and for this a rigid defence was of the utmost importance. Thus a beginning was made even during the mail period towards the introduction of plate-armour. Jazerant and scale armour of small plates had been adopted to this end by the Franks, and Charlemagne had introduced the classic breastplate. Something of the kind was perhaps even known to the Viking, and by the twelfth century Scandinavians certainly used a defence called a briostbiorg beneath the mail, extending from the neck to the waist. Chroniclers allude to shining breastplates long before there is the slightest appearance of them in illustrations, though from the time that surcoats were worn over the armour it becomes difficult to see what is beneath. Allusion is often made to a plastron-de-fer; and in the combat between Richard, when Earl of Poitou, and William des Barres we read that an iron defence was worn over the breast. One of the effigies in the Temple Church is equipped with a back and breast plate of single plates united by straps. It is stated that the bodyguard of Henry III., 400 strong, which fled at the battle of Lewes in 1244, wore breastplates; and in 1277, 300 cavalry so armed were sent to Wales.

Following the head and breast, the limbs received protection from plate-armour, the knees and shins of mounted men-at-arms being peculiarly exposed to injury in melées with infantry, from blows of the two-handed battle-axe and mace. Additional security was absolutely essential against these weapons, which were introduced both for horse and foot by Richard I., and had grown in favour ever since. These even penetrated mail, the Irish axe in particular being reputed to cut off limbs in spite of its protection. The Scandinavians, with their keen military instincts, had provided themselves in the twelfth century with knee-caps of iron attached to overalls worn over the mail. Our earlier mailed effigies, however, show no special defence for the knee, though the one at Salisbury, attributed by Stothard to William Longespée, already noticed, has a stout thong passing between the links of mail just under it. The effigy of Robert of Normandy, of which there is a cast in the National Portrait Gallery, shows a thick overall under the chausses of mail, and drawn over the mail chaussons at the knee (Fig. 8, No. 1), and a similar appearance is seen in the first seal of Richard I.; in the sleeping guards of the Easter Sepulchre at Lincoln (Fig. 9); and other monuments of the same date. In the effigy attributed to William, Earl of Pembroke, in the Temple, who died in 1289 (Fig. 8, No. 2), and in Stothard's drawing of the effigy at Whitworth, an appearance of a thick cap is also to be seen, perhaps the extremity of a padded overall overlapping the knee; and in other examples the thick quilted gambeson leg-defence is clearly seen below the mail, covering the knee, and in the case of De Vere, who died 1221, it has the interesting addition of an octagonal plate (Fig. 8, No. 3), apparently of iron, over the knee-cap. The effigy, called the second Longespée, at Salisbury (Fig. 8, No. 4), about 1260, exhibits an apparently double thickness of mail at this point, caused by the overlapping of the chausses and chaussons, with

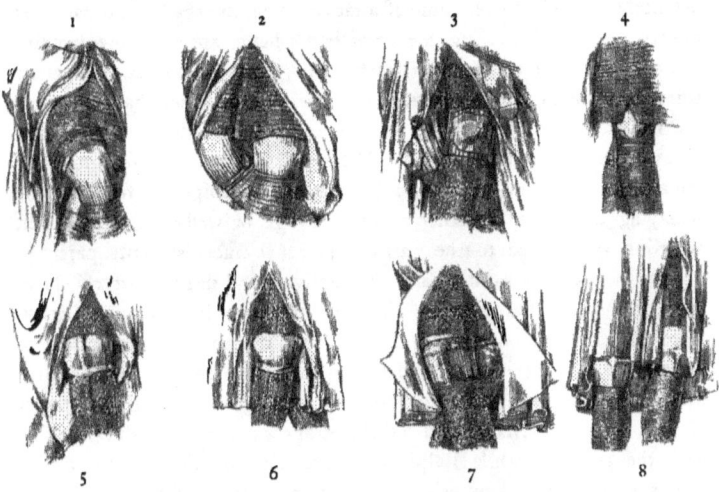

FIG. 8.—*Illustration of the development of plate-armour.*

1. The gambeson appearing below the chausses, but covering the chaussons of mail, forming an extra protection to the knee. From the effigy of Robert of Normandy.
2. The same, but apparently with an extra applied cap. From the effigy ascribed to one of the Pembrokes in the Temple Church.
3. The quilted gambeson appearing below the chausses and drawn over the chaussons, with the additional protection for the knee-cap of an octagonal plate. From the effigy of Robert de Vere, Earl of Oxford.
4. The chausses and chaussons overlapping, forming a double thickness of mail, with the addition of a quatrefoil plate over the knee-cap. From the effigy attributed to the second Longespée at Salisbury.
5. A ridged knee-defence of cuir-bouilli or plate enveloping the knee, over the mail. From the effigy of Robert Ros in the Temple.
6. Globose knee-cap of Aymer de Valence. Westminster Abbey.
7. Decorated knee-defence from an effigy in Whatton Church.
8. Cross-ridged knee-defence from an effigy of Robert de Bois.

the addition of a circular plate with a quatrefoil upon it. Contemporary Chroniclers also mention that greaves were worn by knights in the time of Richard I., though the earliest manuscript illustration of them occurs in Matthew of Paris's *Lives of the Offas*.

The feet were cased in mail, and the spurs were simple straight spikes or goads, perhaps worn on one heel only and called the prick-spur. Under the early Plantagenets the point was fixed on a ball, while the rowel spur is seen in the monument to Le Botiler of the reign of Henry III.

Under the heroic Richard the powers of defence seem to have definitely triumphed over those of attack. Knights sheathed in mail over quilted work, and wearing the great battle-helm, appeared invulnerable and able to encounter the most fearful odds, and even to rescue each other when dismounted amidst swarming enemies. The further changes during the mailed period were in the direction of military display, which has always offered an attractive field. Whenever the pressure for improved armament was relieved through the defensive equipment for the time satisfying the wearer, whether a naked savage or well-equipped soldier, attention was turned to the warrior's personal embellishments, partly to gratify the wearer's vanity, partly to captivate and dazzle, but chiefly to affright and awe the enemy. The fact that the French and English wore the same armour and equipment, and the common occurrence of internecine wars at this time, rendered distinguishing costumes particularly necessary. By simply throwing away their cognisance at the battle of Noyon, Peter de Maule and others escaped recognition and mingled with the pursuers, while Ralph de Courci mistook the French for his own side and was taken prisoner. Nothing but the different-coloured crosses sewn to the garments of the French, English, and Flemish Crusaders served to distinguish them, and white crosses alone distinguished the party of Simon de Montfort, 1264, from their enemies. Nothing approaching to any uniform is heard of in this age, unless when Richard of Gloucester traversed France in 1250, with a retinue of forty knights equipped all alike, with new harness glittering with gold, on his visit to the Pope.

The beautifully-sculptured guards of the early fourteenth century Easter Sepulchre in Lincoln Cathedral (Fig. 9) present fine examples of the costume of the knight armed with the mace, sword, and shield towards the end of the mailed period. The bassinet on the figure to the right is particularly noteworthy.

Fig. 9.—*The sleeping guards, from the Easter Sepulchre in Lincoln Cathedral.*

III

The Transition Period—From about the Reign of Edward I. to that of Richard II., 1272–1399

THE warrior sheathed in mail, mounted on his charger, whether pricking alone or in troops over hill and dale, was a picturesque and portentous figure, and when massed for battle presented an awe-inspiring sight. The gray burnished steel, glittering in the sun or under lowering skies, relieved by the fluttering pennons and banners and emblazoned shields, formed a picture that the old Crusading Chroniclers loved to dwell on, filling the imagination with those great gatherings of the chivalry of Europe. In the days of the last of the Paladins, of Godfrey de Bouillon and Richard Cœur de Lion, the dress of burnished mail was the knight's especial pride, and no garment concealed it. But as progress and love of change are universal, and the mail itself could not well be embellished, an embroidered surcoat was worn over it in the more degenerate days of John and his son Henry, concealing all but the limbs and head. This garment became the vehicle for distinguishing marks and colours, like the modern racing-jacket. A little later, when emblazoned with heraldry, it served to distinguish the individual. The transfer of the surcoat from under to over the mail gave rise to the custom of concealing the steel panoply under rich materials, which distinguished the Transition Period in armour. While it lasted we literally and constantly meet with the "iron hand under the velvet glove." This and the continual piling of one coat of defence upon another, in the fruitless attempt to secure immunity for life and limb, are the chief characteristics of the period we are now to treat.

Until the Transition, the mounted knight, cap-à-pied in mail over the quilted gambeson, with the steel cap, and the great helm for the supreme moment of combat, seemed completely invulnerable unless to missile weapons mechanically projected. Few men-at-arms fell in actual battle on the winning side, and great slaughters were only consequent on the complete rout of one of the parties. Under the warlike Edward I. the powers of attack must have gathered renewed force, for a long period of tentative changes set in which finally ended in the suit of mail being completely hidden beneath an outer shell of steel plates. The qualities of steel for offensive weapons must also at this same time have undergone marked improvements, and we now begin to hear of definite seats of manufacture attaining world-wide celebrity. Cologne, Lorraine, Poitou produced weapons which are said to have pierced mail and quilted armour with ease. The heavy blows given by the battle-axe and mace, used by horse and foot, must, however, have been chiefly instrumental in introducing extra means of defence. These were by no means at first universally of steel, for cuir-bouilli or boiled leather, a very impervious substance when properly prepared, seemed at one time likely to rival it for general use; and trial was made of every other kind of material that could be used for defence, such as horn, whalebone, ivory, padded wool, leather, either alone or strengthened with metal studs or splints, brass, and small plates of iron fixed to textiles. It is almost certain that for a time the moulded surface of cuir-bouilli, with its gilded and perhaps coloured surfaces, was preferred to steel. During this tentative period every combination of these materials with chain-mail is to be met with, and the triumph of steel-plate armour only became definite after every possible substitute, combined in every practicable way, had been tried either at home or abroad and found wanting. It is at least improbable that any armour pictured with enriched designs at this date was of steel.

It would be impossible within the limits of this work, and of little interest, to endeavour to describe the constant changes, often due to individual caprice, that occur; for when groups of soldiery are represented, even long after the Transition, it is rare to find two individuals accoutred in precisely the same manner. We may rest assured, however, that each piece as it successively appears was introduced to meet some new perfection in the weapons of attack, or to cope with some new tactics, in short,

PLATE II.—Second suit of Sir Henry Lee, master of the armoury, reduced fac-simile of No. 19 in the Armourer's Album, in the South Kensington Museum.

to protect some part that had been proved by the practical experience of armed strife to be vulnerable. These additions were naturally subject to modification, according to the passing dictates of military display, or the changing fashions of civilian dress.

Fig. 10 is taken from one of the English MSS. most valuable for the knightly costume of the Transition. The armour is in this MS. almost entirely mail, of the banded variety, worn beneath a surcoat, which is hardly ever emblazoned. Plate-armour is only represented by the knee-caps, with an occasional roundel and shoulder-plate. The great helm, always with a fan-crest, the chapelle-de-fer worn beneath or above the

FIG. 10.—*Melée.*

From the early fourteenth-century English MS. known as Queen Mary's Psalter, 2 B. vii., in the British Museum. The combatants are in banded mail and long surcoats, and some wear the great helms with fan-crests. Ailettes and knee-caps are the only plate-armour visible. Some of the horses have long housings and also bear the fan-crest.

mail coiffe, the bassinet, often visored, and the broad-brimmed round helmet are worn, except in jousts, quite indifferently.

The head, being the most vulnerable part of the body and the most difficult to protect, received the greatest amount of attention. The great helm, with bands and cross-cuts for the sight, continued in use throughout the Transition, but with a sugar-loaf crown, and rendered less insupportable in the reign of Edward I. by transferring the weight from the head to the shoulders. It was occasionally of brass—Chaucer mentions the knight's "helm of latoun bright," a metal used so far back as Henry I.—and much more frequently of cuir-bouilli, as in the tournament at Windsor in 1278, when twelve of the thirty-eight knights had gilded helms, and were called digniores. There can be no doubt, however, that a helm of Poitou steel was even then the surest defence.

To the custom of hanging arms in churches we are indebted for the preservation of all the most valuable historic pieces. The first record of this poetic usage occurs early in the thirteenth century, when William of Toulouse hung his helm and splendid shield over St. Julien's tomb at Brives, and his lance and sword, bow and quiver, outside. By the middle of the century it had become the practice, when a brave knight died, to hang his shield and helm on the walls above his grave, and it appears in addition, from the instance of the King of France after the battle of Cassel in 1328, that the victor in some cases presented his arms to the nearest church. The helm of the Black Prince, still suspended above his tomb at Canterbury (Fig. 11), is an illustration familiar to all. By the kindness of Sir Noel Paton we are enabled to present an even finer helm (Fig. 12), in more perfect preservation, which formerly hung above the tomb of Sir Richard Pembridge, K.G., in Hereford Cathedral, who died one year before the Prince of Wales, in 1375. Its admirable workmanship has been fully described by Baron de Cosson, its fine steely quality being such that no penknife would scratch its polished surface. It is formed of three pieces—the cone, the cylinder, and the top-piece, welded so beautifully that no seam is visible, and these are joined by round-headed nails clinched on the inside. Every practical detail, down to the minutest, has received careful attention. The metal is thickened and turned outwards round the eye-piece, which is thus efficiently guarded, and the bottom edge is rolled inwards over a thick wire, so as not to cut the surcoat. These and other details given by Baron de Cosson in the Catalogue of Armour exhibited at the Royal Archæological Institute in 1880, show conclusively that this specimen at least is a real war helm, fitted to resist and to strike fire under the shock of a lance that might unhorse its wearer. The conical helm was worn over the visorless bassinet next described, as the previous helms had been worn over the chapelle-de-fer, and being only donned in the hour of danger, is rarely represented in monuments, except as a pillow under the head. When worn the face was invisible and recognition impossible, so that a moulded crest of linen, leather, or some light

Fig. 11.—*The helm and crest of the Black Prince, with his shield, from his monument in Canterbury Cathedral.*

material surmounted it and became its most important feature. A mantling was also introduced, at first in the simple form of a puggaree, as seen in the effigy of the Black Prince (Fig. 16), but later of more ample dimensions, fantastically shredded to represent the supposed rents of battle. When the taste for military display increased, these mantles were usually of scarlet lined with ermine. A wide-rimmed helm is often represented as worn over or in place of the bassinet, and jewelled and crested. This form reappears continually, its first introduction dating so far back as the Bayeux tapestry.

The bassinet, used with or without the helm, enjoyed a prolonged period of favour from Edward I. to Henry VI. It differed from the

FIG. 12.—*The helm of Richard Pembridge, K.G., from Hereford Cathedral. Sir Noel Paton.*

FIG. 13.—*Bassinet from the tomb of Sir John de Melsa, Aldborough Church, Holderness. From a photograph by Baron de Cosson.*

older chapelle-de-fer worn with the hood of mail, in having the mail hung round it, instead of passing over or under it. This mail, now called the camail or gorget, was laced to a series of staples along the edges of the bassinet and fell like a curtain on to the shoulders. At the outset merely a skull-cap, it was gradually prolonged at the back and sides so as to leave only the face exposed. Early in the fourteenth century its appearance was profoundly modified by the addition of a movable visor, at first hinged at the side, but subsequently raised and lowered from above the forehead. Being readily removed, the visor was only worn in action, and is thus rarely represented in effigies and brasses. No helm was worn over the visored bassinet, which became the battle head-piece of the fourteenth century and part of the fifteenth, the helm being reserved for jousts and tournaments. We are able, by the kindness of Baron de Cosson, to give an illustration (Fig. 13) of a real bassinet of large size, from the tomb of Sir John de Melsa in Aldborough Church, Holderness. It is described in the Catalogue of

FIG. 14.—*A bassinet transformed into a sallad in the fifteenth century. From Sir Noel Paton's collection.*

Arms already referred to as of the second half of the fourteenth century, and was worn with a large visor. A second bassinet is illustrated (Fig. 14) from Sir Noel Paton's collection, described by Baron de Cosson as transformed into a sallad about the middle of the fifteenth century. Fine bassinets are in the Tower and at Woolwich, and in the Burgess, Christy, and Wallace collections, all happily belonging to the nation, and

C

in Warwick Castle and at Parham, but none are directly connected with English wearers. The beaked visor, represented in so many manuscripts of about the close of the fourteenth century, is a fine defensive and not unpicturesque form. There are several real examples in the Musée d'Artillerie in Paris, two of which are regarded as English.

The bassinet, like the rest of the knight's armour, did not necessarily exhibit a surface of plain burnished steel. It was frequently covered with leather, as mentioned in the inventories of Humphrey de Bohun, 1322, and of Dover Castle, 1344; while the King of France at one time wore his bassinet covered with white leather. One of cuir-bouilli, in Simon Burley's inventory, 1388, is coloured white and green. It was also tinned or gilded, and even of pure gold, as prizes for tourneys, or like one set with gems, sent to Edward I. by his father-in-law in 1334. In a bequest of William Langford, 1411, is a headpiece covered with red velvet, and actual specimens so covered are not unknown. The richness of the decorations bestowed on these helmets is shown in the goldsmith's account of one made for the King of France in 1352, and of another made in the same year for the Dauphin with a band of forty large pearls. Effigies and brasses show that coronets and jewelled fillets commonly adorned them, even in the case of simple knights, and that these are not imaginary decorations may be gathered from Froissart, who mentions that the King of Castille actually entered a battle in 1385 with his bassinet enriched with 20,000 francs' worth of gems. Sir Guy of Warwick, in the Romance, is given a helmet adorned with a circle of gold set with most precious stones.

Some notable champions, like Sir John Chandos and the Earl of Warwick, prided themselves on a disregard of danger and habitually fought without a visor, yet the tendency to close every crevice with plate defences developed continuously, and the frequent accidents at tourneys, when the lance-point glanced upward and entered the throat under the camail, led to the introduction, about 1330, of a gorget of plate or scales, which with the visor converted the bassinet into a closed helmet.

The defence of the breast was always considered next in importance to the head, and fourteenth-century inventories constantly refer to "pairs of plates large," perhaps like those till recently worn in Persia, corsets de fer, cors d'acier, brust plate pour justes, and other defences of plate.

Chaucer writes, "Some would be armed in an haubergeon, a bright breastplate and a gypoun." The globose form given to the chests of effigies, such as that of the Black Prince, seems to imply the presence of a rigid defence under the emblazoned surcoat.

The limbs began to be definitely protected over the mail in the second half of the thirteenth century. Effigies and manuscript illustrations of that date commonly represent globose knee-caps, sometimes ridged down the front, and usually gilt. In the fourteenth century they are always present and frequently treated very decoratively, with shields, roundels, scalloped edges, etc. The technical name for these appendages is "Genouillière," or "knee-cap." Subsidiary plates

FIG. 15.

1. Example of a ridged bassinet with banded camail, from the brass of Sir John d'Abernon, died 1327.
2. Combed and jewelled bassinet from the effigy in Ash Church, of about the same date.

often appear below the knee, and sometimes above it, and are continued under the mail.

The greave was a rigid gaiter fitting at first only over the front of the leg below the knee, but afterwards enveloping it; and it was either of metal or cuir-bouilli. When seen on English fourteenth-century monuments it usually seems to be of steel fitting closely over the mail, and laced or buckled at the back, but at times it is so richly decorated as to suggest cuir-bouilli. Greaves are usually omitted on early monuments, and are only commonly seen when they had become an integral part of the suit of armour. As yet they were not habitually worn except in battle, and knights were not at this time represented in their effigies accoutred for war, but in ordinary military costume. Thus the effigy of Aymer de Valence shows no plate armour, except the genouillière; but the two mounted figures of the canopy present the visored bassinet, the high gorget, the arm and elbow plates, the tubular greaves and steel sollerets for the feet. The tubular leg defence is not seen in earlier representations, and its introduction may coincide with the first recorded appearance in the field of large bodies of Welsh armed with long knives. It was usually hinged and buckled, and becomes more general as the century advances. This appears in the inventory of Piers Gaveston, 1313, who possessed three pairs of such greaves. Monstrelet relates that the bailiff of Evreux, sallying out without his greaves, had his leg badly broken by the kick of a horse.

Defences of plate armour for the feet are called sollerets, and are first, if somewhat indistinctly, visible in the small equestrian figure on the canopy of the tomb of Edmund Crouchback, Earl of Lancaster, in Westminster Abbey, the mail not being continued over the front of the feet as in the older effigies. One of the small equestrian figures of the adjoining tomb of Aymer de Valence has the feet, though mutilated, distinctly covered with small rectangular plates, arranged longitudinally in continuation of the greaves. In the D'Abernon and other brasses of the second quarter of the fourteenth century laminar plates are fastened across the upper part of the foot. Other varieties are the scaled sollerets of the De Cheney brass, 1375; the De Sulney brass, with sollerets of laminar plates, and one large plate over the instep; the Littlebury effigy, with longitudinal plates like those of De Valence. In the effigy of John of Eltham, 1334, we seem for the first time to meet with the whole foot visible incased in plate, as it continued to be during the rest of the century. In the Warwick collection a pair of sollerets are made each of one piece like sabots. The long curved sollerets with pointed toes of the second half of the fourteenth century are called pouleynes or poulaines, from the souliers à la Polaine, and differ slightly from those known as Cracowes, introduced by Richard II. from Bohemia. There are two fine pointed sollerets at Warwick, one measuring twenty-five inches from toe to heel, or with the spur thirty-two and a half inches. Another beautifully-made one attached to leg armour has the plates scalloped along the edges, and is attributed to Edward, son of Henry VI.

The gilt spur was the honorific and distinguishing badge of the knight, and was put on in the ceremony of investiture, and hacked off by the king's cook if the knight was formally degraded. An immense spoil of gilt spurs fell to the victors after the battle of Courtrai. Both the goad and rowel forms were in use throughout the century, and when knights habitually dismounted to fight, they were taken off. Froissart mentions instances where they were fixed in the ground like caltrops. The extravagantly long, rowelled spurs of Henry VI.'s time must have been peculiarly inconvenient.

No great time could well have elapsed before similar defences of plate were found necessary to protect the shoulders and elbows, which were scarcely less vulnerable than the legs. The shoulder-pieces, however, are rarely visible in illustrations and effigies, being much concealed by the surcoat. The earliest arm-defence is in the form of an elbow-guard, and appears in the effigy at Salisbury, date about 1260, consisting of one cupped rosette over another. Elbow-guards are more commonly seen in the second quarter of the fourteenth century, when they consist of cups and discs, or both combined, the latter occasionally spiked. The equestrian figures of the De Valence monument, already mentioned, show in one case gilt rosettes on the shoulders and elbows, and in the other the forearms sheathed in plate. John of Eltham, 1334, has a roundel on the elbow, with articulated plates beneath. In the Ifield effigy the arms are shown by Stothard completely sheathed, and with shoulder and elbow roundels bearing embossed lions' heads. Plain roundels, rosettes, shells, or lion masks were worn on the shoulders, and articulated plates are seen between 1320 and 1350. The singular and exaggerated plates known as ailettes, picturesque objects which rose above the shoulders like epaulettes, were as useless apparently as the shoulder-knots of the present day. They first appear on the scene in the Windsor tournament, 1278, and disappear in the first quarter of the fourteenth century. They are of many shapes and sizes, and are well seen in our illustration (Fig. 10) from Queen Mary's Psalter, in an elegant brass in Weaver's *Funeral Monuments*, as well as in many others, and in several stained-glass windows. Usually they bear the armorial bearings of the owner, though those of Piers Gaveston, 1311, were " frettez de perles."

Mail gloves continued to be worn, though with divided fingers, during the first part of the fourteenth century. The first effigy to show any change is that of a Whatton, engraved by Stothard, of the time of Edward II. Gloves of leather were sometimes worn between 1311 and 1360, as well as others of whalebone, metal studs and splintwork, iron scales and brass. Plate-armour gauntlets first appear towards the middle of the century with articulated fingers and a broad plate for the back of the hand and wrist; whilst a steel cuff, sometimes articulated, was shortly afterwards added. They are at times spiked, or with gads like knuckledusters, as in the case of the Black Prince, and frequently richly jewelled. The jewelled example given from the effigy of Sir Thomas Cawne, of the time of Edward III., is reproduced from Stothard's drawing. The other is from the monument of the Earl of Westmoreland, of the first years of Henry VI. Gauntlets are constantly represented as gilt in MSS. of these periods.

The knight's dress for war now consisted, in addition to any ordinary civilian underclothing, of a more or less complete suit of gambeson or quilted material, sometimes called the haketon, as in Chaucer's *Sir Thopas* :—

> Next his shert an haketon
> And over that an habergeon,
>
> And over that a fin hauberk
> Was all ywrought of Jeweswork,
> Ful strong it was of plate;
>
> And over that his cote-armoure.

The habergeon is the mail in this case, and the hauberk is of plate or splint armour, while the cote-armoure is the surcoat, possibly thickly padded, as in the still-existing surcoat of the Black Prince. In the mutilated effigy at Sandwich the thick quilted gambeson is distinctly seen at the knee and wrist underlying the mail, while the fine hauberk of plate overlies it, and the surcoat is worn over all. The effigy at Ash shows the plate armour, under the surcoat, fashioned in the curious armadillo-like Jazerant or brigandine form, with an upper gambeson under it, as well as the usual second gambeson under the mail. That two separate quilted defences were worn at this time is supported by the De Crell brass, 1325, the D'Abernon brass, 1327, and the Ifield and John of Eltham brasses,

PLATE III.—First suit of Sir Christopher Hatton, Captain of the Guard, and subsequently Lord Chancellor. Reduced fac-simile of No. 15 in the Armourer's Album in the South Kensington Museum.

1334. The colours of these various garments, the edges of which were allowed to show one above the other, were no doubt effectively contrasted, while the edges of the mail, as we have seen, were pinked, vandyked, or scalloped and gilt or finished with brass rings, while the plate-armour finishes most commonly in a fringe-like arrangement of small vertical plates.

The splendid glitter of polished steel, so associated in our minds with the knight in armour, appealed scarcely at all to its wearers in this Transition age. In fact, no decided preference can be discovered even for the defensive qualities of steel, and this constitutes perhaps the most

Fig. 17.

1. Gauntlet from the effigy of Ralph Neville, Earl of Westmoreland, in Staindrop Church, Durham. Time of Henry VI.
2. Gauntlet from the effigy of Sir Thomas Cawne, Ightham Church, Kent. Time of Edward III.

marked peculiarity of the age. In the halcyon days of mail, the steel was kept bright and bare, the helm and shield burnished, with nothing to conceal its brilliancy but a coronet and the rich sword-belts which merely enhanced the effect. But in Chaucer's *Sir Thopas* there is no mention of steel forming part of the visible equipment :—

> His jambeux were of cuirbouly,
> His swerdes sheth of ivory,
> His helme of latoun bright.

Over the body armour was a garment, called by Chaucer "the cote-armoure, as white as is the lily floure."

> His sheld was all of gold so red,
> And thereon was a bores hed
> A charbouncle beside.

The helmets were almost hidden by the large crests and the scarlet mantling, and the metal exposed was generally gilt. The trunk armour was concealed under the emblazoned surcoat or pourpoint; and when the thighs and legs are visible below this they are seen to be clothed over the mail by splinted or brigandine armour, showing velvet or satin externally attached by gilt or silver nails; the knee-caps and greaves are often richly moulded and probably cuir-bouilli, as seen in the statues on the front of Exeter Cathedral, and in the paintings from St. Stephen's Chapel they are also shown as gilt. The arms and at times the hands are similarly clothed. The horse-armour was almost entirely concealed by rich caparisons, as in Chaucer's *Knightes Tale*:—

> Upon a stede bay, trapped in stele,
> Covered with cloth of gold diapered wele.

The figures from the tomb of Edmund Crouchback and Aymer de Valence, engraved by Stothard, show the emblazoned housings of the time of Edward II. The equestrian figures in Queen Mary's Psalter show that the fully-equipped knight of this period, when in full war panoply, was a gorgeous object, blazing in colours and gold, and exhibiting little to recall the stern realities of campaigns and sieges.

A few examples from inventories will best illustrate the colours and the magnificence of the materials used to conceal the steel. Humfrey de Bohun had breastplates covered with "vert velvet"; the Earl of March used "rouge samyt" and "drap d'or," and others had "cendal vermeil, samit vermeil, zatony, veluyau asuré, veluyau vert ouvré de broderie," etc. Piers Gaveston's pair of breastplates were "enclouez et garnie d'argent od 4 cheynes d'argent covery d'un drap de velvet vermail besaunté d'or." Two pairs of plates for the King of France required 3000 crescentic and 3000 round gilt nails to fix the velvet. Exposed pieces of armour were gilt, if not jewelled, pearls and carbuncles being the favourite gems. The baldric, knightly belt, sword-belt, hilt, and scabbard furnished a field for the goldsmith. The magnificence indulged in was often destructive to the wearers, who might have otherwise escaped in battle. They were "hunted for their hides," or slain for the sake of their spoils.

The weight and fashion of the armour largely determined the tactics in war. The English appear at this time to have reverted to their ancient practice, once more dismounting to engage in battle. At Cressy the horses were sent to the rear, while the army, forming into battalions of archers supported by dismounted men-at-arms, took up its ground and waited the attack. The weight of armour carried by the men-at-arms made any forward movement on their part impossible on foot. By good fortune the 15,000 Genoese cross-bowmen, who might have inflicted severe loss on the English, were unable to use their bows, and the French coming up quite out of hand, charged and retreated as the spirit moved them, without deploying into any battle formation, and so fell into the utmost confusion, with the well-known results. Our archers "shot their arrows with such force and quickness that it seemed as if it snowed," piercing the Genoese and dismounting the horsemen; upon which a body of 1000 Welsh foot with long knives advanced through the men-at-arms, who made way for them, and slew numbers of the French chivalry, so that the battle was "murderous and cruel."

At Poitiers, 1356, the English similarly selected a strong position and awaited the attack dismounted. The French, uncertain how to meet the enemy, commenced by attacking with a mounted division, which was routed by the effect of the English arrows on the horses before getting to close quarters. Their retreat threw the second battalion, which also appears to have been mounted, into a confusion, which quickly developed into a panic. Deeming an advance necessary at this critical moment, the English men-at-arms sent to the rear for their horses and charged, completing the destruction and dispersal of all but the rear battalion. This was dismounted in order to fight on foot, and armed with sword and battle-axe presented a most stubborn front, under the king in person, numerous parties from the broken battalions rallying and dismounting to join in its advance. The English resumed the defensive and remained immovable, the archers plying their arrows with the usual effect. The only English force capable of movement and able to skirmish in the field was the archery, while the men-at-arms kept their ground or advanced very slowly in compact order, until, seeing the day won, they again mounted to complete the discomfiture and engage in pursuit.

At the battle of Auray, 1364, the French dismounted and fought on foot, when the arrows did little execution among them, and the fight developed into a hand-to-hand engagement with battle-axes, in which the leaders, Sir Oliver de Clisson and Sir John Chandos, greatly distinguished themselves. In all subsequent battles and skirmishes between French and English, until the close of the century, we find that both sides invariably fought on foot, riding up till almost within striking distance, and then dismounting as if by common consent. To advance any distance on foot after dismounting in order to engage was, in fact, almost impossible. The old knightly weapon, the lance, was in consequence almost discarded, and could now only be used effectively if shortened to about five feet, and thus with the shield fell into disuse as a weapon of battle, while the presence of artillery also began to make itself felt.

IV

The Age of Plate-Armour

ANY line dividing what has here been termed a Transition Age from the age of fully-developed plate-armour must of necessity be a purely arbitrary one. Roughly speaking, the age of plate commenced when mail no longer formed the outer defence of any part of the body. The last chink, leaving the mail exposed under the armpit, was a vulnerable opening in the armour called the "vif de l'harnois," or the "defaut de la cuirasse"; and even this now became protected by small plates of steel called gussets. The necessity for such defences was often proved in tournaments: it is related that the lance pierced "au vif de l'harnois" for lack of the crescent or "gouchet." When these last plates were added the knights appeared more invulnerable than Achilles. We find at almost every period, however, that a fair blow delivered "au pas de charge" with a well-steeled lance might penetrate every defence; and that no armour could be made actually proof against downright blows from a two-handed battle-axe wielded by a powerful and expert rider.

One of the most marked characteristics of this age of plate-armour was a growing appreciation of the intrinsic beauty of steel, and a new desire to invest steel armour with graceful lines. The tendency is best exemplified in the fine Gothic armour of the second half of the fifteenth century, of which much is fortunately preserved. This combines most splendidly picturesque outlines with graceful fan or shell-like ridgings, which please the more when examined critically, since every curve and fluting serves some definite and practical end.

The casing of plate-armour, which had been so long elaborating, having at last become complete, the work of the armourer was directed to further perfecting its parts, and to disencumbering the wearer, with the least risk, of his weighty underlying chain-mail, quilted gambesons, and padded surcoats. This process had not proceeded far when Agincourt was fought, if we may credit the testimony of a French knight, who was present and describes the armour as consisting of the long hauberk of chain-mail reaching below the knee, and very heavy, with the leg-armour beneath, and over this the plate or white armour with the bassinet and camail. One Allbright, noted particularly as "mail-maker," and twelve other armourers, were in the suite of the king on this expedition. The weight of armour would, therefore, have rendered a repetition advisable, on the part of the English, of the tactics of Cressy or Poitiers in this battle, had not the French disconcerted us by dismounting and seating themselves, and refusing to advance. They had also, copying the English, brought a large force of archers and cross-bowmen into the field, and, in addition, kept bodies of men-at-arms in the saddle on either wing, to make flank attacks when opportunities occurred. The English having in vain endeavoured to provoke the enemy to advance by sending out archers to fire a house and barn, posted an ambuscade and moved forward, the archers in front as usual and the men-at-arms behind. The archers thus gave up the shelter of their pointed stakes, and the men-at-arms suffered the fatigue of an advance in armour of an almost insupportable weight to men on foot. They advanced, however, with repeated huzzas, but, as the Chroniclers inform us, "often stopping to take breath." The French, stooping their visors under the amazing hail of arrows that began to fall upon them, gave way a few paces, and the English, coming close up, pressed them soon afterwards so hardly, "that only the front ranks with shortened lances could raise their hands." Our archers, flinging away their bows, fought lustily with swords, hatchets, mallets, or bill-hooks, supported manfully by King Henry and his men-at-arms. Pressing on and slaying all before them, they routed the van and reached the main body, which was also quickly destroyed. The rear battalion of the French, which had remained mounted, then fled panic-struck, and the battle terminated in some desultory charges made by a few parties of nobles and their men-at-arms, which were easily repulsed; 10,000 French perished, all but 1600 being

PLATE IV.—Grand-guard of the suit of George, Earl of Cumberland, in the possession of Lord Hothfield. This is a part of the 20th suit in the Armourer's Album in the South Kensington Museum. From a photograph communicated by Baron de Cosson.

gentlemen! many in the massacre of prisoners consequent on a false alarm. The battle of Verneuil, so fatal nine years later to the Scots, who lost the Earls of Douglas, Murray, and Buchan, with the flower of their army, was fought on precisely the same lines; the main French battalion with their Scottish allies on foot being first shaken by the storm of arrows, and then destroyed at close quarters by the advance of the archers with the usual "loud shouts," supported by the Duke of Bedford and the men-at-arms. These defeats caused the French to again waver in their plan for meeting the enemy, for at the battle of Herrings, and the skirmish at Beauvais in 1430, they made their attack mounted, the English archers receiving the first charge behind their palisade of pointed stakes, and defeating the enemy by the clouds of arrows taking their usual deadly effect on the horses. These stakes, six feet long and sharpened at both ends, formed an important item of the archers' equipment, and were planted in the ground by the front rank, sloping towards the enemy, the next rank fixing theirs intermediately to affright the enemy's horse. Throughout the Anglo-Burgundian alliance, the Burgundians of all arms were often compelled "under pain of death" to fight dismounted, the Picards especially adopting the tactics and perhaps equalling the English. A little later, as at the battle of Montlhery, 1465, both Burgundian and English archers are armed with the formidable long-handled leaden mauls or mallets, which the armour of the men-at-arms was incapable of resisting. In the account of one of these battles we learn incidentally that the duty of the varlets who invariably formed part of the retinue of each man-at-arms was to succour and refresh their masters during the heat of the engagement, and to carry the prisoners they took to the rear.

As the various hauberks of mail, brigandines, gambesons, and other defences became more or less obsolete and discarded by men-at-arms armed cap-à-pied, they were relegated to a lighter-armed cavalry and the infantry; but so long as a suit of mail continued to be worn by the man-at-arms as a defence underlying the armour of plate, flexibility in the latter was of paramount importance.

Regarding the armour of Henry V. as the earliest complete cap-à-pied plate-armour, we find it thus composed. The breast and back plates are each of one piece, the gorget is usually in one, though a standard of mail sometimes replaces it; the limb-defences are of few pieces and rigid, except at the joints, which are guarded by caps or roundels; while the armour of the fingers, toes, and upper surfaces of the shoulders is articulated or protected by narrow laminar plates. The introduction of the gussets, and more particularly of the horizontal bands of plate forming a short petticoat below the waist, materially altered the appearance of the armour of the fifteenth century from that of the fourteenth. The plates of the petticoat, called the tassets, are first seen in the brass of Nicholas Hawberk, at Cobham, who died in 1406, and they gradually increase in number till about 1420. At Agincourt, where the fighting was on foot, the visored bassinet would have been worn by the king and his men-at-arms, and not the great helm. The example of the latter suspended in the chantry of Henry V. in Westminster Abbey, though a real helm, was only purchased from Thomas Daunt, for 33s. 4d., according to Rymer, with the crest, for the funeral. The bassinet was probably plumed with ostrich feathers, which were taking the place of crests, and was encircled by a coronet, damaged in the melée by a blow from the Duke of Alençon, which among its jewels comprised the ruby of the Black Prince, now in the regalia. The diamond-hilted sword was not taken into the fray, unfortunately, as it happened, and fell a prey to the baggage-looters. The king is generally represented wearing a tabard of arms on this occasion, a garment differing from the surcoat in being loose and cut like the modern herald's tabard, emblazoned before and behind and on the broad flaps which do duty for sleeves. The horses, borrowing the custom of Lombardy, wore a heavy chamfron or headpiece of plate, of which a specimen still exists in Warwick Castle, and an articulated crinet or neck-defence of overlapping plates, put together on the same plan as the tassets, and probably some mail defences concealed by the emblazoned caparisons. The ostentatious magnificence which had hitherto covered the body armour of the

FIG. 18.—*Helm from the tomb of Henry V. in Westminster Abbey, date 1400-1420. From a photograph lent by Baron de Cosson.*

knight with silks and satins, velvet and bullion and gems, especially among the Burgundian French, was now in process of being transferred to the horse. The housings are described as of silks and satins of every colour, or velvet crimson and blue, or cloth of gold, and sweeping the ground, besprinkled with escutcheons of arms, and loaded with silversmith's work, or raised work of solid gold. We read of trappings of white silver fringed with cloth of gold, and of cloth of gold interwrought with solid silver ; and it appears that no materials were too rich to deck out the favourite destrier or war-horse. It is unlikely that the English were at this time behind the French in display, for so early as 1409, of the six pages of Sir John de Cornewall, two rode horses covered with ermine, and four horses with cloth of gold ; and in 1414 the English embassy carried themselves so magnificently that the French, and especially the Parisians, were astonished. Splendid, however, as were the housings, the headpieces of the horses eclipsed them. The horse of the Count de Foix at the entry into Bayonne had a headpiece of steel enriched with gold work and precious stones to the value of 15,000 crowns. The Count de St. Pol's horse's headpiece on leaving Rouen was estimated to be worth 30,000 francs, while those of the Dukes of Burgundy and Cleves on the entry of Louis XI. into Paris were still more magnificent. That of the king, however, was on this occasion merely of fine gold with ostrich plumes of various colours. As with the armour in the fourteenth century, the rich trappings of the horse naturally led at times to the pursuit and capture of the owner. It is difficult to believe, in days of such magnificence, that the pay of the Duke of York under Henry V. was only 13s. 4d. per day, an earl received but 6s. 8d., a baron or banneret 4s., a knight 2s., an esquire 1s., and an archer 6d.

Though Henry V. wore royal armour at Agincourt it does not appear that he followed the prudent custom, first noticed in the battle of Viterbo, 1243, of dressing several knights in an identical manner with himself. At Viterbo, on a knight dressed like the emperor being slain, the result was a panic, and the emperor himself had to press with his trumpets into the thickest of the fight to restore confidence. At Poitiers, though nineteen knights were dressed like the king, it did not preserve him from capture. In England, however, the king was saved on many a field by this precaution, as at the battle of Shrewsbury, when the earl,

Sir Walter Blount and two others in royal armour were slain. The passages in Shakespeare will be present to the mind of all :—

> Another king ! they grow like hydras' heads ;
> I am the Douglas fatal to all those
> That wear those colours on them. Who art thou,
> That counterfeit'st the person of a king ?

and again, when Richard exclaims at Bosworth—

> I think there be six Richmonds in the field :
> Five have I slain to-day instead of him.

The appreciation of steel, called by the Chroniclers plain or white armour, for its own sake, had not progressed very far by the time of Henry V.'s invasion of France, but the more lavish splendours were at least reserved for gala occasions. The next modifications were evidently devised to increase the flexibility of the armour, and can be traced with greater precision in England than elsewhere, owing to the fortunate preservation in our churches of a matchless series of military monumental brasses. These clearly indicate that the tendency during the first half of the fifteenth century was to increase the number of joints or articulations in every part of the armour. By the close of the reign of Henry V. things had proceeded so far in this direction that in some cases the greater part of the limb-defences are made up of laminated plates.

The next important change in the appearance of the man-at-arms occurs in the early years of Henry VI., and is due to a striking development of the fan-shaped elbow-guards, first seen in a rudimentary form in 1425, as well as to an addition of short hinged plates called tuilles to the bottom of the hoop-like skirt of tassets which lay closer to the body. By 1435 these tuilles are ridged or fluted perpendicularly and scalloped along the lower edge, and shortly after they take the more developed, elongate and elegant forms familiar in Gothic armour. By 1440 we have the addition of great shoulder and elbow plates attached by nuts and screws, and concealing the articulated shoulder-pieces or epaulettes. These extra plates usually differ in size, being often very much larger on the left side, which received the blows, and thus conferring a quite peculiar character on the plate-armour of the middle of the century. A scarcely less important modification, introduced about 1445, is the articulation of the breastplate in two pieces, the lower overlapping and sliding over the upper, and made flexible by straps.

The Daundelyon brass of this date, at Margate, exhibits a left elbow-piece of immense size, and pointed and ridged tuilles below the tassets, which are almost repeated again in form by the plates below the knee-caps. John Gaynesford's brass at Crowhurst, 1450, presents strong reinforcing shoulder-guards over articulated plates, and repeats the same long peaked and ridged plates below the knee-cap. We continue for the next few years to find the limb-defences constantly varying in the number and form of the pieces composing them, according to the dictates of conflicting requirements, namely flexibility and impenetrability. The frequent absence of tuilles at this time is held to imply that they were not used in combats on foot, then very popular. It is obvious that when the immensely long and pointed solleret came in with the equally preposterous spur, the fashion of fighting on foot was on the wane, and the men-at-arms generally fought mounted during the Wars of the Roses.

We see by manuscript illustrations that a few suits were still gilded, and we find Jack Cade after his victory in 1450 flourishing about in a suit of gilt armour, the spoils of Sir Humphrey Stafford. But the ever-growing appreciation of the intrinsic beauty of the steel panoply and its fine military qualities is now distinctly felt, and the armourer sought more and more to invest his work with beauty of form. All is still entirely dictated by fitness to its purpose, and the requirements of jousts and war; and the decorative and subtle shell-like ridgings and flutings are really present more to deflect the weapon's point than as ornament, while the engrailing, dentelling, scalloping and punching of the margins of the plates unmistakably indicate that the decorative spirit is applied to embellishing and not to concealing the steel. The superb gilded metal effigy (Fig. 19) of Richard Beauchamp, Earl of Warwick, presents a faithful model of the most beautiful type of Gothic armour known. Every fastening, strap, buckle or hinge is represented with scrupulous fidelity, not only on the front, but on the unseen back. Baron de Cosson, who has minutely described it, expresses the belief that it is a faithful reproduction of a suit actually worn by the Earl, and therefore earlier than 1439; although the effigy itself was only produced in 1454, and the armour agrees with that worn in England at the latter date. He regards the suit represented as the work of the celebrated contemporary Milanese armourers, the Missaglias. Italian armour is shown by sculptures, medals and paintings to have been many years in advance of English, and the two known contemporary suits by Tomaso di Missaglia greatly resemble it. The Earl of Warwick knew Milan in his youth, when he had tilted successfully at Verona; and it was a practice among the great to obtain armour there, dating from so far back as 1398, when the Earl of Derby had his armour brought over by Milanese armourers; the Baron's view presents therefore no improbabilities. Wherever made, the Earl of Warwick's suit appears to have solved the armourer's problem, being at once light, flexible, yet impenetrable. Indeed, in its beautiful proportions and admirably perfect adaptation to all requirements, it appears more like a work of nature than of art. The contours of the pieces and their graceful fan-like flutings, to give strength and deflect opponents' blows, are artistically splendid. The great shoulder-guards and elbow-pieces, the cuissarts and winged knee-caps, the tuilles, the jointed breast and back plates, the upright neck-guard, not hitherto seen, are all fashioned with consummate skill. In such a suit the preux and gallant knight for three days held his tournament victoriously against all comers, presenting each of his discomfited adversaries with new war-chargers, feasting the whole company, and finally "returning to Calais with great worship." The two cuts (Figs. 20 and 21), illustrating scenes from his life, are taken from the exquisitely drawn illustrations to the contemporary Beauchamp manuscript, now in the British Museum. The incidental testimonies to the excellence of Italian armour of the middle of the fifteenth century are abundant. A stalwart Burgundian champion tried in vain during a tournament in 1446 to penetrate or find a crevice in the armour of the Duke of Milan's chamberlain, whom it was impossible to wound; and in 1449 the suit of another knight in the service of the same Duke was said to be steeped in some magic liquid, as so light a harness could not possibly have otherwise withstood the heavy blows it received.

No word ever escapes the chronicler in praise of English armour; but the splendid model of the Earl of Warwick's suit is by William Austin,

founder, and Thomas Stevyns, coppersmith, both of London, with the gilding, chasing, and polishing by Bartholomew Lambespring, Dutchman and goldsmith of London. The will directs that the effigy shall be made according to patterns, directions obviously most scrupulously carried out.

In contemplating the lithe figure we may well believe that the steely quality and workmanship of such a suit would confer immunity

FIG. 20.

The Earl of Warwick slays a "mighty Duke" who has challenged him to combat for his lady's sake, and wins the favour of the Empress, to whom he makes a present of pearls and precious stones. The costume is about fifteen or twenty years later than the death of Earl Richard, and shows the extra pieces worn in the tilt-yard, 1450-60.

on the wearer; and that the relative elasticity and lightness of a perfectly-fitting suit might confer such superiority on an active and sinewy champion engaging with men swathed like mummies beneath their armour in thick gambeson or mail, as to enable him to emerge from his deeds of arms as triumphantly as the heroes of romance. Nothing was worn beneath but the fustian doublet, well padded and lined with satin, with the small lozenge-shaped gussets of mail under the limb-joints and the short petticoat of mail tied round the waist. It is also unlikely that such armour was concealed under any garment, and we may observe that while some princes and nobles are still wearing brigandines of velvet and cloth of gold in pageants, many more are in "plain armour," presenting, except when standing collars of mail were worn, a uniform surface of smooth polished steel.

The Missaglia suit remained the type with little modification for several years, almost to the close of the Gothic period. The Quatremayne brass in Thame Church, of the year 1460, presents a magnificent example of it with singularly exaggerated elbow-guards. During the next few years the limb-pieces and gorget become more articulated and flexible, and the breast and back plates are formed of as many as three or four overlapping articulated plates, cut chevron-wise, and notched and indented in an interesting manner. The gauntlets and sollerets are also of excellent workmanship. There are a number of peculiarly fine examples in the Museum of Artillery in the Rotunda at Woolwich, from the Isle of Rhodes, which exhibit the graceful outlines and ornament of later fifteenth-century Gothic armour in perfection, and also present early and interesting examples of engraving on armour. Lord Zouche has also some remarkable suits, said to be from the Church of Irene at Constantinople, in his collection at Parham. Sir Noel Paton's fine collection also comprises several Gothic suits, and there are some in the Tower. None, however, are connected historically with English wearers, and the destruction of Gothic armour in this country appears to have been unusually complete. The illustrations from the *Life of the Earl of Warwick*, an English MS. of the second half of the fifteenth century (Figs. 20 and 21); and the scene (Fig. 25) from the late fifteenth-century MS. of Froissart, which belonged to Philip de Commines, both now in the British Museum, give excellent ideas of the armour of this period in actual use, while the brasses supply exact figures of the details.

Turning now to head-defences, the great crested helm, still represented as pillowing the head in effigies, had long since been relegated to the joust and tilt, while the bassinet with a visor, already seen in the Transition period, remained the fighting helmet till about the middle of the century. The visor, however, was not unfrequently struck or wrenched off in tourneys, and the neck pierced by the lance. Some hardy warriors, indeed, like Sir John Chandos and the Earl of Warwick, dispensed with it and went into the fray with faces bare, but this was

FIG. 21.

The Duke of Gloucester and Earls of Warwick and Stafford chase the Duke of Burgundy from the walls of Calais. They wear loose sleeves and skirts of mail, and the round broad-brimmed helmet very fashionable for a time among the higher French nobility. The balls and tufts are probably Venice gold, with which the helmet was perhaps also laced, over some rich material. This and Fig. 20 are from the Beauchamp MS. in the British Museum, an exquisite production by an English hand.

exceptional, and the pig-faced and beaked visored bassinets occur in all delineations of combats of the first half of the century.

The bassinet began to be superseded towards the middle of the fifteenth century by the sallad, which remained in fashion almost to its close. Its merits were, the free supply of air it afforded, and the readiness with which the face could be concealed and protected. It was the headpiece of the Gothic armour, such as that of the Warwick effigy, though monuments of this date almost always leave the head bare. The origin of the sallad, whether German or Italian, is unknown, but the term occurs in Chaucer. In its simplest form it was low-crowned, projecting behind, and strapped under the chin, something like a "sou'wester" or the heraldic chapeau, and in this form it was worn by archers and billmen. Another kind had a higher crown, with two slits in front as an ocularium, and could be pulled over the brows till this came level with the eyes (Fig. 22). A hinged nose-piece was also sometimes present, to be let down in time of danger. It was also made more completely protective by a chin-piece called the bavier, strapped round the neck or fastened to the breastplate for tilting; while a lighter bavier was in two pieces, of which the upper was hinged at the side and could be raised for speaking. It was frequently furnished with a visor to let down. The tail-piece was occasionally so prolonged that sallads measure as much as eighteen inches from back to front. It occurs both smooth-topped and combed, and with a slot for plumes approaches nearer to classic models than any other form of mediæval helmet. This picturesque headpiece is the one so frequently represented by Albert Dürer, and was favoured for a longer time in Germany than elsewhere, many of the Germans in the picture of the meeting of Maximilian and Henry VIII. appearing in it, while all the English wear the later close helmet or armet. The form represented has the addition of articulated pieces behind and a double visor moving on pivots at the sides, which make it a near approach to a closed helmet.

The sallad was the principal helmet in use throughout the Wars of the Roses, and is constantly represented in manuscripts of that period. But one solitary example has been preserved in England from the time of those destructive wars, in which its first wearer may have taken part. It hangs in St. Mary's Hall, Coventry, and owes its preservation to its use as a stage property in the Godiva processions. There are specimens, however, in all the important collections in England and abroad.

PLATE V.—Grand-guard, used for tilting, belonging to the suit of Robert Dudley, Earl of Leicester, with the gilding restored. In the Tower of London

The bassinet was sometimes richly decorated, covered with velvet, plumed, crested, and of considerable value, Sir John de Cornwall wagering his helmet in 1423, which he offered to prove to be worth 500 nobles. The pretty custom of garlanding them with may, marguerites, or other flowers specially favoured by a queen or princess, or with chaplets of pearls and other gems, seen in the early part of the century, lasted until after the introduction of the sallad, which provided a better field for such display. A sallad belonging to the Duke of Burgundy, decorated with rubies and diamonds to the estimated value of 100,000 crowns, figured in the entry of Louis XI. into Paris in 1443. In the expenses of Henry VII. precious stones and pearls are bought from the Lombards to the value of £3800 for embellishing sallads and other helmets, and in France even the sallads of the mounted archers are continually mentioned as garnished with silver.

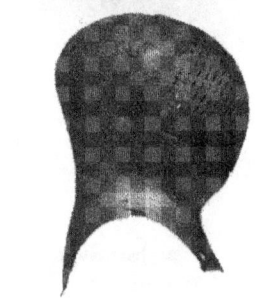

Fig. 22.

1. Sallad in St. Mary's Hall, Coventry.
2. Helm of Sir Giles Capel, date 1510-1525. Formerly in Rayne Church, Essex. Now in the possession of Baron de Cosson.

The sallad was a relatively dangerous headpiece in tourneys on foot, and a large-visored bassinet is often mentioned as being retained in use for this purpose down to the sixteenth century. The Baron de Cosson has identified this form, seen to have been fixed to the breast by two staples and a double buckle behind, and himself possesses a magnificent example, which once hung over the tombs of the Capels in Rayne Church. Sir Giles Capel was one of the knights who with Henry VIII. challenged all comers for thirty days on the Field of the Cloth of Gold. The visor in this example is very massive, the holes so small that no point could possibly enter, and the helm being fixed the head moved freely inside. A second and possibly earlier example has the visor thrown into horizontal ridges and a small bavier. The visor is hinged at the sides, and the sight and breathing holes are short slots, parallel to and protected by the ridges. It hangs over the tomb of John Beaufort, Duke of Somerset, in Wimborne Minster, who died in 1444, but it is of later date; and another belonging to the suit of Henry VIII. in the Tower, made for fighting on foot, is not dissimilar. Baron de Cosson calls attention to the fact that this form, called a bassinet, is shown in the miniature of the manuscript entitled, "How a man shalle be armyd at his ese when he schal fighte on foote."

Fig. 23.—*English tournament helm over the tomb of John Beaufort, Duke of Somerset, in Wimborne Minster. Weight 14¼ lbs. Date 1480-1520. From a photograph lent by Baron de Cosson.*

Another very interesting and thoroughly English form of helm, intended, according to De Cosson, for the tilt with lances, is preserved in a specimen in Broadwater Church, another in Willington Church over Sir John Gostwick's tomb, and a third in Cobham Church, the helm of Sir Thomas Brooke, who died 1522. These all present considerable differences of detail. A not dissimilar helm of slightly later date with a barred visor, or the bars riveted to the helm, affording plenty of breathing space, was used for the tourney with sword or battle-axe, and has become the Royal and the nobles' helmet of heraldry.

A form of helm used for tilting with the lance and also frequently depicted in heraldry, is the great helm of the time of Henry VII. and Henry VIII., of immense weight and strength, resting on the shoulders, and securely fixed to the back and breast. It was relatively flat on the crown, produced in front into a kind of blunt beak, giving a bird-like aspect with no distinct neck. The ocularium, or slit for vision, is large and in the crown, and can only be used by bending the body forward; the head being raised before the moment of impact to avoid the danger of the lance penetrating. This helm is well represented in the tournament roll of Henry VIII. in Heralds' College, and from its massive strength and the fact that by no possibility could a combatant be accidentally unhelmed, afforded absolute protection to the head. Le Heaulme du Roy is represented in this roll as silvered, with a crown-like border round the neck of pearls and gems set in gold. There is a magnificent specimen in the Museum of Artillery at Woolwich, one in Westminster Abbey, two in St. George's Chapel, one in Petworth Church, and one at Parham. This form of helm was the most massive and secure, and the last that remained in use. A very early delineation of a helmet of this type is seen in the late fourteenth-century French MS. (Burney, 257) in the British Museum. Some exceedingly interesting delineations of the same kind of tilting helm in actual use are to be seen in Philip de Commines' Froissart, Harl. MS., 4379-80 (Fig. 25). It is there represented plain and fluted, and with various crests and mantling, one of the most singular, and a favourite, being a close copy of the lady's head-dress of the period, with the lady's long gauze veil reaching below the waist. This manuscript is of late fifteenth-century date, and very remarkable for the apparently faithful representations of the armour worn by the English and French at that time. In one group of soldiery alone, in the second volume, page 84, the helm of the early fourteenth century, the beaked bassinet of the early fifteenth, and various forms of visored and un-visored sallads are assembled together.

FIG. 24.—*Helm of Sir John Gostwick, died 1541.*

Believed to have been worn at the Field of the Cloth of Gold, 1520, and now hanging over his tomb in Willington Church, Bedfordshire. From a photograph by the Rev. Augustus Orlebau, Vicar.

All these forms of helm were more or less contemporary with the sallad, which gave place in turn to the armet or closed helmet, first heard of in 1443. Like, perhaps, the sallad, the armet was invented in Italy, and did not reach England or even Germany till about 1500. In France, however, a page of the Count de St. Pol bore a richly-worked armet on the entry into Rouen of Charles VII.; and the royal armet of Louis XI., crowned and richly adorned with fleurs-de-lis, was carried before him on his entry into Paris in 1461. It is also mentioned in 1472, in an edict of the Duke of Burgundy.

The fundamental difference between it and all helms and helmets that had preceded it is, that while others had either fitted the top of the head, as a cap does, or were put right over it, the armet closed round the head by means of hinges, following the contour of the chin and neck. Its advantages were neatness, lightness, and general handiness, and it conveyed the weight by the gorget directly on to the shoulders. Its use was exclusively for mounted combatants, though the great helm continued in use for jousts and tilts during the time of Henry VIII. It does not appear in English costume much before this reign, but in all the pictures of the triumphs and battle-pieces of Henry VIII. at Hampton Court, the English men-at-arms invariably wear it, and it is abundantly represented in works of art during the remainder of the Tudor period.

An early armet, identified by Baron de Cosson as Italian, with a double bavier riveted together, but without a visor, hangs over the tomb of Sir George Brooke, eighth Lord Cobham, K.G. (Fig. 26), and dates from 1480 to 1500. Baron de Cosson describes it as having a reinforcing piece on the forehead, hinged cheek-pieces joined down the middle of the chin, and of peculiarly delicate and beautiful outline. It originally had a camail hanging to a leather strap. The wooden Saracen's head may date from the funeral of this Lord Cobham in 1558, "but was certainly never worn on any helmet." Its owner served under Norfolk in Ireland, in 1520, and was subsequently Governor of Calais.

English armets dating from about 1500 are not uncommon, but, as frequently observed, "they want that perfection and delicacy to be found in fine Italian or German work." The earlier open down the front, and the later at the side. They are generally combed, the ridge or comb

FIG. 25.—*The entry of Queen Isabel into Paris in 1390.*

The knights wear the great tilting helms, and the foremost has a copy of the ladies' head-dress for crest, from which depends a fine lawn veil. The housings are embroidered with gold. From the Philip de Commines copy of Froissart, Harl. MS. 4379, vol. 1, fol. 99, in the British Museum, late fifteenth century.

running from the forehead to the back of the neck, and being beaten or raised out of the metal in the most able way. There is generally, but not always, a reinforcing piece over the forehead. The visor is of one piece, and works on a pivot, but in a few of the early specimens the pin and hinge arrangement of the older Italian examples is preserved, rendering it removable. The slit for vision is generally made in the body of the visor, but is sometimes obtained by cutting out a piece of its upper edge. It is beaked, thrown into few or several ridges, with the slits or holes for breathing principally on the right side. The English armet was rarely furnished with a bavier or movable chin-piece, and the fixed one, called a mentonière, was small. Baron de Cosson obtained one from Rayne Church in Essex, when it was pulled down, and Meyrick procured a similar one from Fulham Church, and Mr. Seymour Lucas, A.R.A., has two very fine specimens, now exhibited at South Kensington, while specimens are to be met with in most great collections. The not inelegant fluted Maximilian armets of the same date are, however, far more frequent. Like the later English armets, they have no baviers. Between 1510 and 1525, a hollow rim was introduced round the base of the helmet, fitting closely into a corresponding ridge round the upper edge of the gorget. This manifest improvement was considered by Meyrick to constitute the

FIG. 26.—*Armet of Sir George Brooke, K.G., 8th Lord Cobham. From his tomb in Cobham Church, Kent.* 1480-1500.

FIG. 27.—*English armet from the collection of Seymour Lucas, A.R.A. Date about 1500. From a photograph by Baron de Cosson.*

E

Burgonet. Between 1520 and 1540 the visor was formed of two parts, the upper of which closed inside the lower, and was capable of being raised without unfixing the latter. It remained in this form until the closed helmet fell into disuse in the seventeenth century. The armet frequently comprised, especially in the later examples, a fixed gorget, generally of two or more articulated plates. A number of these are included in the sixteenth and seventeenth century suits illustrated in the succeeding pages, one of the most singular being the helmet of the mounted suit of Henry VIII., made for the king by Conrad Seusenhofer of Innsbrück in 1511-14. It consists of six pieces fitting one within another without hinge or rivet, and seems originally to have had one of the curious discs at the back seen in Italian fifteenth-century armets and contemporary illustrations.

Towards the beginning of the sixteenth century knightly armour underwent some profound modifications. The exaggerated elbow-guards and shoulder-pieces were reduced, the tuilles, the laminated corselets with their handsome flutings and indented margins, and the pointed sollerets were either modified or seen no more; and with them disappear much of the angulated, defensive mannerism, and the grace peculiar to the armour of the third quarter of the fifteenth century. That which followed appears smoother, rounder, and heavier, less mobile, and less apt for real campaigning. The modifications tending to this result may have been in a large degree due to the personal tastes of the three great monarchs of Europe. Maximilian and Henry VIII. preferred at heart the pomp and pageantry to the realities of war; while the classic bias of Francis I. banished all Gothic feeling so far as his personal influence extended. The short-waisted, podgy, globular breastplate, the stolid limb-pieces, rounded knee-caps and strikingly splay-footed sollerets, appear as if invented to altogether banish the very idea of agility, if not of movement; and contrast in the strongest manner with the lithe and supple-looking armour of the Beauchamp effigy. The Tower collection, so relatively poor in Gothic armour, is fortunately extremely rich in that of the period of Henry VIII., containing four or five suits actually made for his personal use. One of the finest of these, and an admirably perfect suit, is shown in our illustration (Fig. 28). Though without any decoration or marks, it was undoubtedly made expressly for the king,

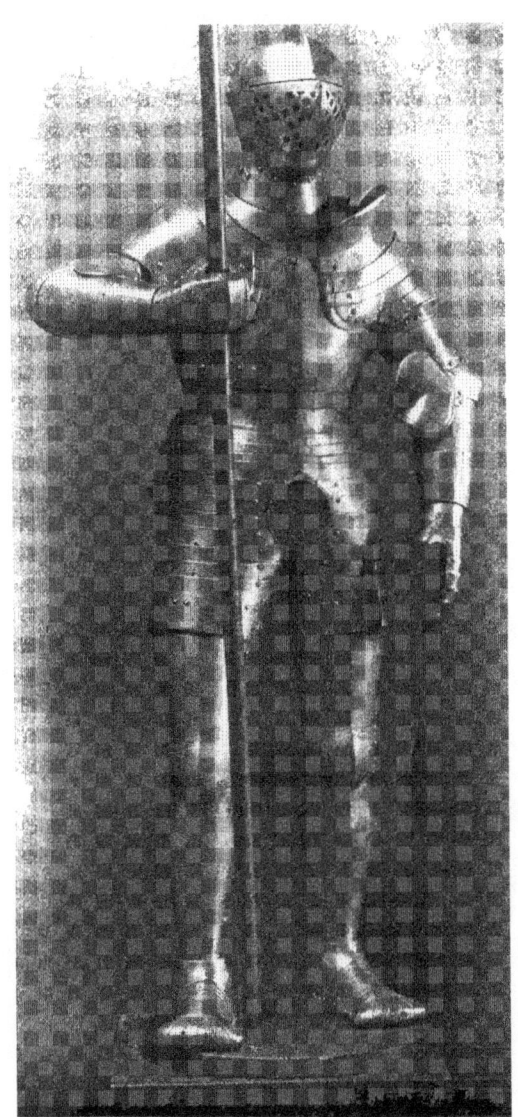

FIG. 28.— Complete suit for fighting on foot, made for Henry VIII. In the Tower of London.

and is a chef-d'œuvre of the armourer's craft, being formed, according to Lord Dillon, of no less than 235 separate pieces, which are used about one half below and the rest above the waist. The principal pieces are fitted with a hollow groove along the inferior margin, and overlap others provided with a corresponding ridge: so that the whole suit thus interlocks, and the plates cannot be separated or the armour taken apart except by removing the helmet and beginning at the neck-pieces. To the left shoulder-piece or pauldron one of the upright neck-guards is still fixed by rivets. The breastplate is globose, and has a central ridge called the tapul. The arms are sheathed in rigid plates, separated by a series of narrow laminar plates, by which power of movement is obtained. The elbows are guarded by not inelegant caps, and the gauntlets are miton-fashioned, of eleven small plates, and very flexible. The leg-armour is in large pieces ridged down the centre, similarly to the breastplate, except above and below the knee-cap, and at the ankle, where laminar plates give the necessary play. The sollerets being made, like the gauntlets, each of thirteen pieces, are also extremely flexible, and reproduce in an exaggerated way the great broad toes of the civil dress. Like the helm, already noticed, the suit is intended for combats on foot and in the lists, which were greatly in fashion. No mail gussets were needed, for there were no crevices between the plates, and the wearer inside his armour was as well defended as a lobster in its shell; but this security, as with all armour-plate, was purchased, notwithstanding the perfection of manufacture, at the expense of unwieldiness and fatigue, for the suit weighs over 92 lbs. There are three other suits which belonged to Henry VIII., besides the magnificent equestrian one next figured. The second dismounted one was also intended for combats on foot, and is known as a tonlet suit from the long, laminated skirt of horizontal plates reaching to the knee, and sliding over each other. It is decorated with some engraved bands or borders, while the fine headpiece to it is Italian, bearing the marks of the celebrated Missaglias of Milan. We meet at this time with the sliding rivets, a new mode of attachment for the plates, which enabled them to play freely over each other without parting company. The overlapping tassets of most of the close-fitting skirts are made in this fashion, to which the term Almayne rivets, so frequently met with in inventories, is believed to apply. Some of the suits are provided with a locking gauntlet, to prevent the sword from being struck out of the wearer's hand, the so-called forbidden gauntlet, though its prevalence in collections negatives the idea that its use was disallowed. In one mounted suit the insteps are protected by the great ungainly stirrups necessitated by the broad-toed sollerets, and therefore only covered with mail. This suit is enriched with a picturesque banded ornament, partly gilt.

The superbly-mounted suit in our illustration (Fig. 29), one of the finest of its date in existence, was constructed to the order of Maximilian expressly for Henry VIII., by Conrad Seusenhofer, one of the most celebrated armourers of Innsbrück, whose mark it bears on the helmet. It was sent as a gift in 1514, and was originally silvered all over, and finely engraved in every part with the legend of St. George and the badges of Henry VIII. and Katharine of Arragon. The Tudor cognisances are the rose, portcullis and red dragon; and Katharine's the pomegranate and sheaf of arrows, with finely-scrolled arabesque work between. This ornament seems to be engraved and not etched, as in later times. The most remarkable feature is the steel skirt called base, of great rarity, and made in imitation of the folds of the cloth bases so much in vogue at this time. These skirts were used for fighting on foot, and there is provision for fixing an additional piece to complete it in front, the absence of which alone permitted the wearer to sit on horseback, though the difficulty of getting into the saddle must have been considerable. The skirt is edged with a finely-modelled border of brass in high relief, with the initials H. and K. united by true-lover's knots. The suit is complete in every respect except the gauntlets, and is mentioned in the Greenwich inventory of 1547, published in the fifty-first volume of *Archæologia* by Lord Dillon. It is there described as "a harnesse given unto the King's Maiestie by Th^e Empero^r Maximilian w^t a Base of stele and goldesmythes worke." The brass border to the base thus appears to have been regarded as silver and gilt goldsmiths' work. The horse armour matching the suit, which was to be used on foot, as Lord Dillon points out, did not exist at this period, and the figure was seated on the Burgundian horse armour of repoussé steel of the time of Henry VII., which still stands next

FIG. 29.—Suit made for Henry VIII. by Conrad Seusenhofer of Innsbrück, 1511-1514. A present from the Emperor Maximilian I. In the Tower.

to it in the Tower. The engraving on the horse armour or bard is designed in the same spirit as that of the armour itself, but is by an inferior hand. The subjects are treated in the style of Albert Dürer or Burgkmair, and represent incidents in the lives of St. George and St. Barbara, and besides the badges on the armour which are reproduced, the castle and the rose and pomegranate impaled appear, with the motto DIEV ET MON DROYT many times repeated round the edge. All these badges and engravings were illustrated, almost real size, by Meyrick, in the twenty-second volume of *Archæologia*. The horse armour was silvered and probably parcel gilt, like the body armour, and was made, it is supposed, by some of the German armourers brought over and established in Greenwich by Henry VIII. It is stiff and unwieldy, and does not very efficiently protect the horse, though its effect is dignified and even magnificent. The singular construction of the helmet has already been alluded to.

Contemporary with these suits is the fine German late Gothic fluted armour, known as Maximilian, nearly perfect examples of which are to be seen in every collection of importance. This was used for tilts, with the immensely massive outwork of plates to fend off the blows of the lance and other weapons, and to prevent the left leg from being crushed against the barrier. Some of the rarer Maximilian suits not only reproduce the cloth skirts of the civil costume in steel, but also innumerable puffings and slashings, which were the fashion of the day. Sometimes the helmets belonging to these suits have the mask-shaped visors, a specimen of which, also a present to Henry VIII. from Maximilian, still exists in the Tower. This formed part of a tilting harness, and is described in the 1547 inventory as "a hedde pece w^t a Rammes horne silver pcell guilte." In 1660 it was attributed to Will Sommers, the king's jester, and has subsequently been rendered more grotesque by paint and a pair of spectacles. A complete helmet of the same kind is preserved at Warwick Castle, as well as one of the rarer Italian helmets, with curling woolly hair represented in embossed iron, but without the visor.

All this armour was made for the shocks and pleasurable excitement of jousts, tilts, and tourneys, which its perfection and strength deprived of nearly every element of danger. Its weight and closeness would indeed have made it insupportable on active service. The great revolution in the equipments for war, commenced by the artillery train and nearly unarmoured pikeman and estradiot, was now being completed by the reiter, pistolier and arquebusier. The massed man-at-arms, armed cap-à-pied, had borne down for the last time all before him with the lance, and was ceasing to play a decisive or even an important part in warfare. Armour in campaigning was becoming of little consequence, and even for the tourney a reaction was setting in against the extravagant and ponderous precautions devised by Maximilian and his admirer Henry.

The decision of battles now belonged to pike, bill, and musket. The infantry and light troops, who had hitherto been left to arm themselves as best they could, began to be dressed in some sort of uniform, with weapons and armour selected with some care, and used in definite proportions. It is certainly strange to read that the archers who did such splendid service at Agincourt were left to pick up any kind of helmet, bassinet, or cap, whether of leather or wicker bound with iron, and any description of side-arms, and were mostly without armour, save the pourpoint, with stockings hanging down or bare feet. Only the bows, arrows, and stakes were obligatory. In pictures, archers and the foot generally are represented in every kind of old brigandine, mail, bits of plate, or "jakkes" of linen, which inventories tell us were stuffed with horn or mail. It was only when the kings and nobles thought it worth their while to clothe and equip the foot-soldier that his costume became distinctive, and even sumptuous in the case of the bodyguards to Charles VII., Louis XI., or Henry VII. and VIII. A larger proportion of archers became mounted as the fifteenth century wore on, Edward IV. invading France with no less than 14,000, besides the foot. Picked men, and those of the bodyguards of kings and princes, like the Duke of Burgundy, were sometimes magnificently dressed. The uniform of the archers of the Duke of Berri in 1465 was a brigandine covered with black velvet and gilt nails, and a hood ornamented with silver gilt tassels. At the entry into Rouen, 1460, the archers of the King of France, the King of Sicily and the Duke of Maine wore plate-armour under jackets of various colours, with greaves, swords, daggers and helms rich with silversmiths' work. The leaders of other corps were in jackets striped red, white and green, covered with embroidery. English archers are sometimes spoken of as gallantly accoutred. Under Henry VIII. the bodyguard called the "retinewe of speres" comprised two mounted archers in uniform to each man-at-arms, as in France. Every layman with an estate of £1000 and upwards had to furnish thirty long-bows, thirty sheaves of arrows, and thirty steel caps. In 1548 the uniform of the English archer was a coat of blue cloth guarded with red, right hose red, the left blue, or both blue with broad red stripes, and a special cap to be worn over the steel cap or sallad, to be bought in London for 8d. They were provided with brigandines or coats of little plates, mawles of lead five feet long, with two stakes, and a dagger. The distinguishing mark of the various bands was embroidered on the left sleeve. In 1510 Henry ordered 10,000 bows from the bowyers of London, and applied for leave to import 40,000 from Venice. In 1513 he took 12,000 archers to France, and in 1518 agreed to furnish 6000 archers to the emperor. In this reign they did good service, as in repelling the descent of the French at Brighton, 1515, and at Flodden, where the King of Scots was found among the dead pierced by an arrow. Some bow-staves of yew were recovered from the wreck of the *Mary Rose*, and are now in the Tower. At Dover Castle there are a long-bow and a cross-bow, stated to be part of the original armament.

The cross-bow was rarely favoured by Englishmen, though an imposing force of 4000 appeared in the united forces of England and Burgundy in 1411, each attended by two varlets to load, so that the weapons were always ready to shoot. In 1415, however, Henry V. only took ninety-eight from England in his whole force of 10,500 men, eighteen of whom were mounted. In 1465 the so-called mounted archers were very variously armed in France, with cross-bows, veuglaires, and hand culverins.

If so formidable a body as the English archers could be left to their own devices as to accoutrements in the first half of the century, the rest of the foot, armed with long weapons called staves, bills, and halbards, must have presented the appearance of a mere rabble. The French foot, armed with partisans, halbards, or javelins, bore the suggestive name of "brigans," and were much despised, but at Montlhéry in 1465 the greater part of the slaughter was by the "rascally Burgundian foot," with their pikes and other weapons tipped with iron.

The Swiss victory at Morat in 1476 undoubtedly led the French, and later the English, to introduce a disciplined infantry armed with the pike as a serious element into the army. In 1480 the French took the extreme course of disbanding the whole body of archers, substituting Swiss pikemen, and causing a prodigious number of pikes, halbards, and daggers to be made by the cutlers. Thus in 1482 the army of Picardy is composed of no more than 1400 men-at-arms, 6000 Swiss, and 8000 pikes. The proportions in England, ten years later, may be gauged by the Earl of Surrey's contingent of five men-at-arms, each with cushet and page, twelve demi-lances, twenty archers mounted, forty-six on foot, and thirteen bills. The archers remained an important force with us till long after Henry VIII., but it is only in his reign that the billmen and halbardiers occupy a definite position in the country's armed forces. These were armed with bill, sword, shield, sallad, and corselet. The costume of the foot and even the yeomen of the guard, 1000 strong under Henry VIII., changed with the civil dress, but always included the royal badge and crown. Henry proceeded to the siege of Boulogne in the midst of his pikemen with fifty mounted archers on the right and fifty mounted gunners on the left. Their costumes are seen in the Hampton Court pictures. In 1598 it was scarlet profusely spangled. Under Philip and Mary they were an even more important force, and under Elizabeth the backbone of the army was its pikemen, billmen, and harquebusiers, now armed, as in France, with Milanese corselets and morions. The bill was six feet long, of native production, the head at least twelve inches long, and bound with iron like the halbard, which was shorter, to at least the middle of the staff. The black bills were also shorter and from Germany, but the best halbards were Milanese. The partisan with us seems to have been more a weapon of parade, various in form, with or without wings, and richly decorated with engraving, painting, and gilding. The pike was eighteen to twenty-two feet long, with a tassel to prevent the water running down. The "Staves" in the Tower under Henry VIII. included 20,100 morris pikes, some highly decorated, and 2000 javelins, mostly richly mounted, as if for the Court guards. The army taken to France in 1513 comprised, according to the Venetian ambassador, 6000 halbardiers and 12,000 men with holy-water sprinklers, a weapon never seen

PLATE VI.—Profile of the helmet belonging to the French suit (fig 32). In the guard-chamber of Windsor Castle.

before, six feet long, surmounted by a ball with six steel spikes. The name was a quaint joke, like the Flemish Godendag or the Swiss Wasistdas and Morgenstern. Besides these there were tridents, pole-axes, collen cleves, boar-spears, rawcons, partisans, and other forms of staff weapons in smaller quantities.

An English army sometimes comprised light cavalry even in the earliest times, perhaps none more singular than a miserably-accoutred force of mounted Irish armed with target, short javelin, and great outlandish knives, but without using saddles, in the reign of Henry V. The army of Henry VIII. in 1513 comprised 9000 to 10,000 heavy barbed cavalry and 8000 light horse, and 2000 mounted archers. His " Retinewe of speres" comprised a page, a cushet with javelin or demi-lance, and two archers, all mounted, to each man-at-arms. An English force of about 400 demi-lances serving Henri II. in 1552 "for their pleasure," were in short petticoats, red bonnets, body with brassarts of plate, and high leather boots above the knee, mounted on swift little horses and armed with a lance like a demi-pike.

The infantry, though not yet a permanent standing force, except in the case of the Royal bodyguards, was now a recognised arm into which men enlisted as a professional career for the term of their lives or until disabled. To handle the pike or arquebus efficiently required long training, and veterans were always accepted before recruits. It was their steadiness and power of manœuvring in action that lessened the value of heavy cavalry, and consequently contributed, more than any other circumstance, to the rapid disuse of the cap-à-pied suit of armour in the field, so noticeable in the next chapter.

V

The Age of Enriched Armour

ARMOUR began from about the accession of Edward VI. to cease to be a military necessity, and those engaged in practical warfare were more ready to dispense with its doubtful protection than to encumber themselves with its certain disadvantages. Excuses were found for appearing in the field without armour, or with an imperfect equipment, and punishments were inflicted in the vain attempt to stem the tide of change. Those who served on foot had naturally the strongest objection to bearing its weight, since when opposed to firearms it ceased to have any practical utility. A battle-scene at Hampton Court, the battle of Forty by Snayers, furnishes the strongest justification for its disuse among men-at-arms. It represents a number of mounted men in complete armour, who discharge horse-pistols point blank at each other's breast-plates, the individual struck falling in every case dead or wounded from his horse. The wheel-lock pistol, the arm of the German Reiters, who wore black armour, mail sleeves, and a visored morion, was in the field in 1512. From this time, therefore, armour was worn rather for display than service, and the purchaser came to value its defensive qualities far less than the magnificence of its decoration. Nor was ostentation in arms confined to the noble or knight alone. Brantôme says that among the pikemen and musketeers of Strozzi, De Brissac, and the Duc de Guise, thousands of gilt and engraved morions and corselets were to be seen on parade days, and the armour worn by the picked force of Spaniards and Italians sent by Philip of Spain to occupy the Netherlands was a splendid sight. The great and wealthy have seldom

FIG. 30.—*Part of a suit made for Sir Christopher Hatton.*

From the Spitzer collection, and now in the possession of Mr. Charles Davis. This is No. 15 in the Armourers' Album in the South Kensington Museum, reproduced in our Plate III.

cared to stint in matters of personal adornment, and in days when there were fewer ways in which a taste for extravagant expenditure could be combined with a high appreciation of art, fortunes were spent upon the coverings of the body. Nothing more sumptuous in applied art exists, in regard either to design or execution, than the work lavished on the armour produced for the French, Spanish, and other monarchs in the second half of the sixteenth and beginning of the seventeenth centuries. Among this the most exquisitely beautiful is the damascened work, scattered over Europe, persistently though erroneously attributed to Cellini, of which, perhaps, one of the finest examples is the target at Windsor. It is no exaggeration to say that neither chiselling, embossing, nor damascening on metal has ever rivalled or even approached that bestowed at this time upon royal arms and armour. The chief seats of production were in Germany and Italy, at Milan above all, then Innsbrück, Augsburg, Nuremberg; and in a less degree Florence, Brescia and Venice. It is singular that few fine suits can be attributed to France, and fewer still either to Spain, the Netherlands, or England. The youth of Edward, the fact that female sovereigns succeeded, and finally, the timidity and horror of war felt by James, account for none of the known chef-d'œuvre suits being made for English wearers. Such extraordinary and magnificent armour was meet for none but the high-spirited and rival princes of Europe, and no king distinguished for valour occupied the throne of England during the period when enriched armour reached its culminating point of grandeur.

There are, however, a certain number of richly engraved and gilt suits which have been in the possession of English families from time immemorial, and the fortunate acquisition for the South Kensington Museum Art Library of an Armourers' Album of the time of Elizabeth, has enabled many of the original wearers of them to be identified. This MS., as Lord Dillon relates, was in the possession, in 1790, of the Duchess of Portland, daughter of Harley, Earl of Oxford, who permitted Pennant to engrave from it a suit of Robert Dudley, Earl of Leicester, for his account of London; while Strutt was allowed to reproduce that of George, Earl of Cumberland, for his work on dresses and costumes. The book undoubtedly once formed part of the great Harleian Library, but was lost until seen in Paris some years ago by Baron de Cosson. It

F

was sold at the Spitzer sale, acquired by M. Stein, and offered to the Kensington Museum, by whom it was wisely purchased.

The drawings are in pen and ink and water-colours and represent twenty-nine full suits, besides the extra pieces for tilting. Some of them are inscribed "Made by me Jacobe," the name of the master armourer at Greenwich during part of Elizabeth's reign, and mentioned by Sir Henry Lee, the Master of the Armoury, in a letter to the Lord Treasurer, dated 12th October 1590, published by Lord Dillon in the fifty-first volume of *Archæologia*. Wendelin Böheim, the curator of the Imperial collections of armour at Vienna, has recently identified this Jacobe with Jacob Topf, one of three brothers, natives of Innsbrück or its vicinity, and who suddenly appears as court armourer in 1575. This post he seems to have retained and worked at Schloss Ambras till his death in 1597. Suits made by him during this period for the Archduke Ferdinand of Tyrol and Archduke Charles of Styria certainly bear some resemblance to those in the Album. Böheim infers from the Italian influence seen in his work, especially in the ornament, that Topf must have proceeded from the atelier of Jörg Seusenhofer to Milan or Brescia, about the year 1558, and taken up his abode in England between 1562 and 1575.

To support the identification of the Jacobe of the Album with Jacob Topf of Innsbrück, it is necessary either that all the suits should have been produced before 1575, or that those made at a later time should be regarded as by some other hand. The first two, for Rutland and Bedford, who died respectively in 1563 and 1564, are relatively plain, and have M.R. over them, and the rest E.R., which can only, it would appear, have reference to the initials of the reigning queens. All the figures are practically drawn from one model, though sometimes reversed, and are in an easy and graceful pose. Two of the richest, namely the second suit for Sir Henry Lee, the Master Armourer, No. 19, and the first suit of Sir Christopher Hatton, No. 15 of the Album, are here reproduced in facsimile, though reduced in scale (Plates II. and III.). One holds a mace and the other a truncheon in one hand, with the butt resting upon the hip, while the other arm is bent and the extended palm rests upon the thigh. They wear the close helmet or armet of Italian fashion, with a high comb and a large sharply-pointed visor. The gorgets are laminated, the

Fig. 31.—*Armour of Robert Dudley, Earl of Leicester, 1566-1588. In the Tower.*

pauldrons large and massive, the breastplates long-waisted, known as the peascod shape, ending in a point, with a ridge down the centre called the tapul; the tassets are short and laminated. Only the front of the thigh is protected by laminated cuissarts, and the rest of the leg by close-fitting knee-caps and greaves. The sollerets are complete and take the shape of the foot. The swords appear to be simply crosshilted and worn in scabbards. Both the suits reproduced are richly engraved with vertical bands of gilt arabesqued ornament in the Italian fashion: Sir Christopher Hatton's being on a russet ground with a gold corded pattern connecting the bands; and Sir Henry Lee's on a white ground with a knotted reticulated pattern between. The minor details are considerably varied in the other suits, two of which have been reproduced by Lord Dillon, and two by Böheim in the publications already referred to. The complete list comprises the names of many of the leading nobles and captains of Elizabeth's reign, only two in it being foreigners.

The ornament is sufficiently distinct to admit of the suits being identified where they still exist. Thus the Earl of Pembroke's suit is still at Wilton, in perfect preservation; the suit of George, Earl of Cumberland, is in the possession of Lord Hothfield at Appleby Castle. The grand-guard of this suit, with volant attached, forms the subject of Plate IV., in which the original russet and gilding is somewhat restored. The ornament on the bands is an interlacing strap upon a foliated arabesque ground, with a figure of Mercury near the top, and two E's at intervals addorsed and crowned, coupled by a true-lover's knot. Between are large roses and fleurs-de-lis united by knots. The helmet of Sir Henry Lee's second suit, Plate II., is now in the Tower, having been identified by Lord Dillon, while a locking gauntlet belonging to it is in the Hall of the Armourers' Company. This gauntlet, called the "forbidden gauntlet," was in form of a closed right hand, the fingers fastened by a hook and staple, leaving an aperture for the passage of the weapon which, if a lance, or sword with cross-guard and pommel, could not be dislodged. In the Tower are also the vamplate of Sir Christopher Hatton's second suit, and the complete armour of the Earl of Worcester, with both the headpieces. A helmet of Lord Sussex's suit is in the Tower, and two gauntlets belonging to it were in the Spitzer sale.

Lord Bucarte's suit is in the Wallace collection at Hertford House, and another fine suit is in Armourers' Hall.

The first Sir Christopher Hatton suit, Plate III., has also recently reached this country, fortunately in almost perfect condition. It was disposed of in the Spitzer sale, and was purchased by Mr. Davies of New Bond Street. It will be a misfortune if this historic piece is not added to the national collection. Fig. 30 represents the upper part of this suit, taken from a photograph, with the high neck-guards attached to the pauldrons. The original front-plate seems to be lost, but the extra breastplate for tilting and some other extra pieces are preserved.

If Boheim is correct in his identification of Jacobe with Jacob Topf, and in his dates, the armour in the Album must be by different hands. Thus Topf, arriving in 1562, could hardly have made the first two suits marked M.R., the owners of which died, as we have mentioned, in 1563 and 1564 respectively. The mail defence for the instep and the relatively broad toes are features of an earlier time, which the letters M.R. identify as that of Mary, and show that the very broad stirrup of Henry VIII. was still in use. Neither could he, being settled in Innsbrück or at Ambras in 1575, have made the suits for Sir Henry Lee, as Master of the Armoury; nor that for Sir Thomas Bromley, as Lord Chancellor, though the latter suit may have been for Sir Nicholas Bacon, the previous Lord Chancellor. The chief difficulty is the date of Sir Henry Lee's appointment, which Lord Dillon in his able treatise, in the *Archæological Journal* for June 1895, gives as 1580, and the fact that the solitary mention of Jacobe in any document is by Sir Henry Lee himself, and is dated October 1590, in which he speaks of him as "the M^r workman of Grenewhyche," and in a way that could not well have reference to one who had quitted the post fifteen years before. These difficulties may, however, it is possible, yet be reconciled.

Among the fine suits in the Tower is the equestrian armour of Robert Dudley, Earl of Leicester (Fig. 31), not however one of the suits in the Album. It is, like the Jacobe suits, banded in the Italian fashion, with a similar kind of design upon the bands, and between them a broad impressed diaper of crossed ragged staves and leaves filled with fine arabesques. Among the enrichments can also be seen the George of the Garter,

Fig. 32.—*A superb suit of French armour in perfect preservation. Early seventeenth century. In the Guard-chamber of Windsor Castle.*

the bear and ragged staff, the initials R.D., and the collar of the Order of St. Michael and St. George, conferred upon this favourite of Queen

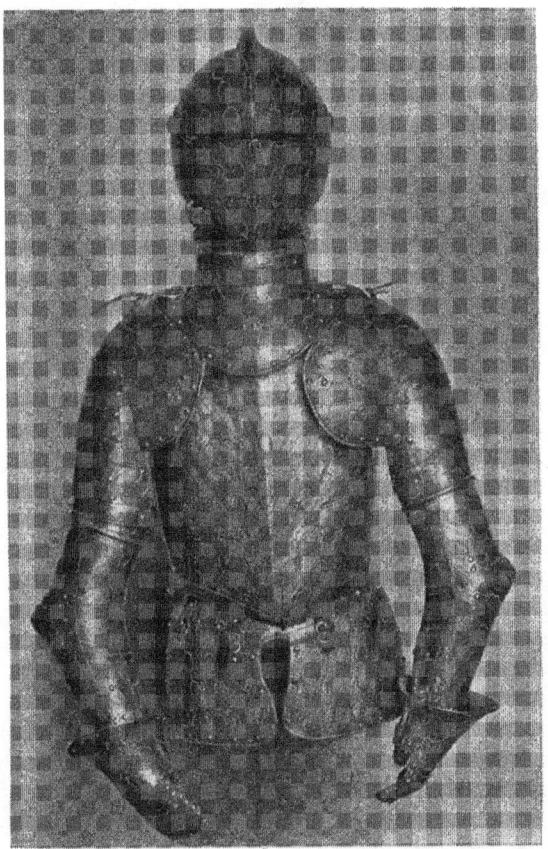

Fig. 33.—*Italian suit of blued and gilded steel covered with appliqués of gold. In the Guard-chamber of Windsor Castle.*

Elizabeth in 1566. In the illustration of this suit, Fig. 31, the bear and ragged staff is plainly visible on the horse's chamfron, from which issues a twisted spike. The armet is combed, but differs in form from the Jacobe type, and the visor is pierced on one side with round holes. In other respects the fashion of the armour is very similar to that of his enemy, Sir Christopher Hatton. The grand-guard and pass-guard or elbow-guard are preserved with it. The former is illustrated, Plate V., with its original gilding restored, the military cleaning and scouring to which it has been subjected for so many years, not wisely but too well, having obliterated every trace of the original splendour of colour. A portrait of the Earl in this very suit exists, however, to show what it was. He died, it is well known, in 1588.

Several splendid and historic suits are preserved in the Guard-room at Windsor Castle. Among these, one, the suit of Prince Henry of Wales, son of James I. (frontispiece), bears a remarkable resemblance to the Jacobe suits, recalling especially the design of the Cumberland suit, Plate IV. But for the alternation of thistles among the fleurs-de-lis and roses between the bands of gilded ornament, the body armour in both would be nearly identical. The monogram H.P. appears on the gilt bands of strap and arabesque work. The gilding is in fine preservation, and except that the steel was formerly a deep blue, in the Milanese fashion, it is still as represented in the portrait of Prince Henry in the possession of the Marquis of Lothian. It has been attributed to William Pickering, Master of the Armourers' Company of London in 1608-9, on the faith of some payments made to him, which Mr. St. John Hope has noted as follows: "In March 1613, a warrant issued under sign manual, for the payment to Sir Edward Cecil of a balance of £300 due for armour value £450 for the late Prince Henry: and in July 1614 a warrant issued to pay William Pickering, Master of the Armoury at Greenwich, £200 balance of £340 for armour gilt and graven for the late Prince." The helmet somewhat resembles that of the Leicester suit, but has a singularly stiff, vertically-ridged gorget with scalloped edge, and heavier gauntlets. The leg-defences and sollerets do not differ appreciably from those already noticed. A number of the extra pieces and some of the horse armour belonging to the suit are preserved with it. If really by Pickering he was a close copyist of Jacobe. An apparently companion suit of Prince Charles is looked on with suspicion by Lord Dillon. Another of Prince Henry's suits,

PLATE VII.—Ornament on the tapul of the breastplate belonging to the half-suit of the Earl of Essex, (fig 35) with the original gilding slightly restored. In the guard-chamber of Windsor Castle.

presented by the Prince de Joinville, and now in the Tower, was originally of blued steel richly ornamented with classical designs in gold. There are also in the Tower a fine suit made for Charles I. when a boy, some silvered pieces, and the richly gilt and engraved armour presented to him by the City of London.

FIG. 34.—*A part of the ornament of the Italian suit (Fig. 33), drawn real size.*

Another suit at Windsor of extraordinary magnificence is that represented in Fig. 32. It is, unfortunately, not well set up, and differs considerably in construction from those hitherto noticed, and is of later date than the Jacobe suits. The tassets are replaced by laminar cuissarts extending to the knee, below which the suit is not continued. The ornament is banded vertically, like that of the suits previously figured, but is of a richer character. Its details and colouring are reproduced on a larger scale in the helmet, Plate VI., which is combed, fluted, and of singularly graceful outline, with all its fastenings, plume-holders, and the stiffly-ribbed gorget in most perfect condition. The whole appears to be a specimen of rare French armour, but nothing is known of its history. Even more sumptuous, if possible, is the Italian suit, Fig. 33, which also exhibits some peculiar characters, such as the single plates in place of the tassets and the construction of the arm-defences and gauntlets. The setting up in this suit is also unfortunately defective. The extraordinary richness of the damascening and appliqué work is reproduced in Fig. 34, in which a portion is sketched real size. Nearly all the escutcheon-like appliqués have been picked off at some period, either for mischief or for the gold. The original owner of this suit is also unknown, but it may, with the one last described, have possibly been a present to Prince Henry, whose passion for military exercises and display is matter of history. The last of our illustrations (Fig. 35) taken from suits in the Windsor Guard-chamber is a demi-suit of the Earl of Essex, and is a war suit, something like a pikeman's, except that the closed helmet was not worn by dismounted men. This is combed, and introduces a shade or peak over the sight. It has no visor, but a bavier in two pieces protects the face. It should perhaps be described as a burgonet with gorget and movable mentonières. Probably only a part of the suit is present, that for use on foot, and the helmet may belong to the missing equipment for a rider, or if worn on foot it would have been as an open burgonet. The Jacobe Album introduces us to the burgonet and cabasset, a lighter morion, and shows that these were used when fighting on foot by even the greatest captains. This suit is also decorated in bands, a fashion almost universal during the reign of Elizabeth. The breastplate is the peascod with tapul form, and the cuissarts "à écrivisse" form the only protection for the legs. The ornament is more finely and delicately chased than that of any suit yet noticed. The design on the bands is an interlacing and knotted strap, filled with arabesqued foliage enclosing medallions with emblematic figures and flowers encircled by mottoes, as Futura præteritis, on a ground etched down, but with foliage and bright points like grains of seed, left on it. A part of this ornament is drawn full size in Plate VII.

Fig. 35.—*Demi-suit of the Earl of Essex, with closed helmet, magnificently engraved and gilt. From the Guard-chamber at Windsor Castle.*

There is a suit in the Tower attributed to the same Robert Devereux, Earl of Essex, who was executed in 1601, also richly engraved and gilt.

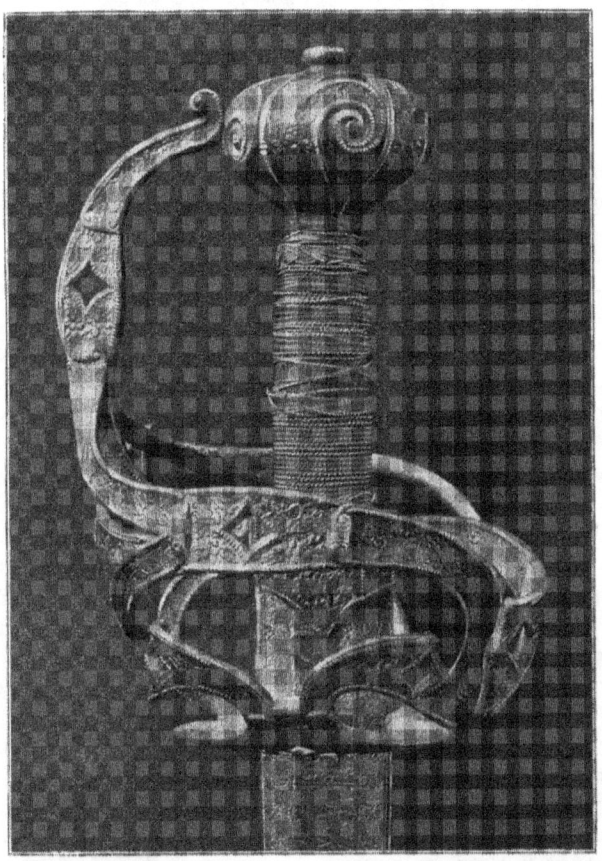

Fig. 36.—*Sword, probably of James I., with basket hilt, entirely covered with raised gold damascening. Preserved in Windsor Castle.*

The suits now divided between Windsor and the Tower evidently formed part of a single collection. Those at Windsor are placed on brackets at such a height that they can only be inspected from a ladder, and they sadly require setting up, in the way that Lord Dillon has mounted those in the Tower. It is perhaps unfortunate that the national collection of armour is so scattered, parts being, besides the great collections at the Tower and Windsor, in the British and South Kensington Museums, Hertford House, Woolwich Rotunda, and Dover Castle, while most of the earlier English and historic pieces are still in churches and cathedrals. If brought together, properly displayed and added to in a reasonable manner by the purchase of such suits as that recently sold in the Spitzer sale, a suit of fine quality and directly connected with our national history, it might become worthy the country, and rank in time with the great armouries of Vienna, Paris, Madrid, Turin, or Dresden.

Besides the half-dozen really magnificent suits in the Guard-chamber at Windsor, there is a vast collection of arms and weapons in the North Corridor, formed in a great measure by Her Majesty. Among these are three swords intimately connected with our history. Of these, that of Charles I. has a pommel and guard of steel overlaid with raised gold damascening, and a grip covered with silver wire woven like basket-work (Plate VIII.). The blade is decorated with Latin inscriptions in Roman capitals along both margins, back and front, and in circles at intervals. Between these are panels, alternately of emblems and ornament, and of arabesqued scrolls, damascened so minutely that the work is almost invisible until magnified. The small portion of the blade in our figure shows the character of the work. The royal arms, Prince of Wales' feathers, and date 1616 on the blade show that it was made for Charles I. when Prince of Wales. The second sword, with the magnificently-worked basket hilt of chased gold inlay on steel (Fig. 36), has a similar blade, marvellously fine arabesques taking the place of the marginal inscriptions. It is otherwise nearly identical with the last, the spread eagles, griffins, etc., being common to both. The presence of the lion of England under a royal crown points to James I. as its owner. The third sword (Fig. 37) is that of John Hampden. Its blade is plain, but the hilt is of superb workmanship and of carved steel. The grip is small, and, like the pear-shaped pommel, covered with warriors in relief in Roman dress. The quillons are slightly curved, and carved with

PLATE VIII.—The sword of Charles I. when Prince of Wales, 1616. The hilt entirely covered with raised gold damascened work on blue steel matrix; except the grip of silver wire work. Preserved in Windsor Castle.

pomegranates and foliage, with figures reclining horizontally to form the extremities. The smaller front guard over the blade, known as the

Fig. 37.—*The sword of John Hampden, with hilt of carved steel. Preserved at Windsor Castle.*

"pas-d'âne," and most elaborately worked with figures and medallions, is a prominent feature of the hilt. All three swords bear the unicorn's head mark of Nuremberg, but the two enriched blades can be identified, thanks to the assistance of Baron de Cosson, as the work of Clemens Horn of Solingen, 1580-1625. There is a similar sword in the Royal Armoury at Madrid, belonging to the suits made by Desiderius Kolman for Philip II., and another is in the Baron's own collection. The sword, as the emblem of knightly honour and faith, was from the remotest times a vehicle for the richest decoration; but it is doubtful whether any specimens were ever produced, even by the combined efforts of the swordsmith and jeweller, to equal the work of those here represented, which are not only connected with the history of our country, but happily also the property of the nation.

INDEX

D'Abernon brass, 36, 40
Acre, Siege of, 14
Agincourt, Battle of, 46, 48, 49
Aldborough Church, 33
Alençon, Duke of, 48
Alfred, King, 10
Allbright (armourer), 46
Almayne rivets, 70
Appleby Castle, 85
Archæological Institute, 30
Archers, 17, 20, 43, 46, 47, 58, 74-76
Armet, The, 58, 62, 65, 66, 82, 90
Armourers' Album, 81, 82, 86, 92
Armourers' Hall, 18, 86
Arthur, King, 7, 10
Ash, Effigy at, 40
Athelstan, 10
Augsburg, 81
Auray, Battle of, 44
Austin, William (armourer), 52

Bacon, Sir Nicholas, 86
Badges, Heraldic, 20
Barres, William de, 22
Base, The, 70
Bassinets, 24, 29, 30, 32-34, 36, 46, 48, 56-61
Battle-axes, 45
Bavier, The, 58, 62, 65, 92
Bayeux Tapestry, 12, 32
Beauchamp, Richard. *See* Warwick, Earl of
Beauchamp MS., 52
Beauvais, Battle of, 47
Beche, De (monument), 19
Beckman, 18
Beowulf, 9-11
Bills, 46, 76
Black Prince, The, 30, 32, 35, 40, 48
Blount, Sir Walter, 50
Böheim, Wendelin, 82, 85, 86
Bohun, Sir Humphrey de, 34, 42
Boileau, Etienne, 18
Boulogne, Siege of, 76
Bourgthéroude, Battle of, 14
Bows and arrows, 14, 43, 74
Brantôme, 78
Breastplates, 7, 22, 34, 35, 42, 47, 51, 52, 66, 69, 85, 86
Brescia, 81, 82
Brigandine, The, 42, 47, 56, 74, 75
British Museum, 6, 7, 10, 18, 52, 56, 61, 96
Brives, 30
Broadwater Church (helmet in), 60
Bromley, Sir Thomas, 86
Brooke, Sir George, 62
Brooke, Sir Thomas, 60
Bucarte, Lord, 86
Burgess Collection, 33
Burgonet, The, 65, 92
Burley, Simon, 34
"Byrnies," 9, 18

Cabasset, The, 92
Cade, Jack, 51
Camail, The, 32, 46, 62
Cambray, Battle of, 16
Canterbury, 30
Canute, 11
Capel family, 59
Caractacus, 7
Cassel, Battle of, 30
Cassivelaunus, 7
Cawne, Sir Thomas (effigy of), 40
Cellini, Benvenuto, 81
Chain-mail. *See* Mail armour
Chamfron, The, 48, 89
Chandos, Sir John, 34, 44, 56
Chapelle-de-fer, The, 20, 29, 30, 32
Chariots, 5, 7
Charlemagne, 22
Charles VII., 62
Charles Stuart, Prince, 90, 91
Chausse and Chausson, 22, 23
Cheney, De, brass, 36
Christy Collection, 33
Clisson, Sir Oliver de, 44
Clypeus, The, 5
Cobham, 48, 62
Cognizances, 24
Commines, Philip de, 56, 61
Comnena, Anna, 12-14
Cornewall, Sir John de, 49, 58
Corselets, 66, 78
Cosson, Baron de, 30, 33, 51, 59, 60, 62, 65, 81, 98
Courci, Ralph de, 24
Courtrai, Battle of, 39
Coventry (sallad at), 58
Cracowes, 36
Crell, de, brass, 40
Cressy, Battle of, 43, 46
Crests, 20, 21, 29, 30
Crinet, The, 48
Crossbows, 14, 15, 43, 75
Crossbow-men, 16, 46
Cuir-bouilli, 28, 29, 34, 42
Cuissarts, 52, 85, 91, 92
Cumberland, Earl of, 81, 85

Damascened armour, 81
Danes, The, 12
Danish armour, 10
Daundelyon brass, The, 51
Daunt, Thomas, 48
Dillon, Lord, 20, 69, 70, 81, 82, 85, 86, 90, 96
Diodorus Siculus, 6
Dover Castle Collection, 18, 34, 75, 96

Easter Sepulchre, Lincoln, 22, 24
Edda, The, 11, 18
Edward I., 15-17, 32, 34
Elbow-guards, 39, 50, 52, 56, 66
Enamelling on bronze, 5-7
Enriched armour, 78-81
Epaulettes, 50

Essex, Earl of, 92, 95
Ethelwulf, 10
Evans, Sir John, 5
Evesham, Battle of, 14
Exeter Cathedral, 42

Falkirk, Battle of, 14
Flint, 7
Flodden, Battle of, 75
Florence, 81
Fluted armour, 73
Foix, Comte de, 49
Fram, The, 8
Francis I., 66
Frisian Pirates, 8
Froissart, 34, 39, 56, 61

Gambeson, The, 16, 19, 23, 28, 40, 46, 47, 55
Gardner, Mr. J. E., 18
Gauntlets, 39, 40, 56, 69, 70, 85, 90, 92
Gauntlets, Forbidden. *See* Gauntlets, Locking
Gauntlets, Locking, 70, 85
Gaveston, Piers, 36, 39, 42
Gaynesford, John (his brass), 51
Genouillière. *See* Knee-cap
Gildas, 8
Gilded armour, 7, 30, 40-42, 51, 73, 91
Gisors, Battle of, 15
Gloucester, Richard of, 24
Godwin, Earl, 11
Gordon, Adam (outlaw), 16
Gorget, The, 32, 34, 36, 56, 62, 65, 82, 90, 92
Gostwick, Sir John, 60
Grand-guard, The, 85, 90
Greaves, 23, 35, 36, 42, 74, 85
Gussets, 45, 48, 55, 69

Habergeon, The, 40
Haketon, The, 40
Halberds, 75, 76
Hampton Court, 62, 76, 78
Hanging arms in churches, 30
Harold, 12
Hastings, Battle of, 12, 14, 15, 20
Hatton, Sir Christopher, 82, 85, 86, 90
Hauberk, The, 16, 18, 19, 40, 46, 47
Hawberk, Sir Nicholas, 48
Helmets, 7, 12, 20, 28, 29, 32, 33, 34, 42, 56-66, 90, 92
Helm or Heaume, The Great, 20, 24, 28, 29, 48, 56, 60, 61, 62
Henry I., 14, 16
Henry II., 16
Henry III., 16, 20, 22, 24
Henry V., 46-50, 75
Henry VI., 32, 50
Henry VII., 59, 60
Henry VIII., 58-62, 66, 69, 70, 73-77

835

INDEX

Henry Stuart, Prince, 90, 92
Hereford Cathedral, 30
Herrings, Battle of, 47
"Holy-water sprinklers," 76, 77
Hood, Robin, 16
Horn, Clemens (armourer), 98
Horse-armour, 15, 42, 49, 73, 90
Housings, 49

IFIELD effigy, 39, 40
Innsbrück, 81, 82, 86

JACOBE (armourer), 82, 86, 90-92
John of Eltham (his effigy), 36, 39, 40
John, King, 15
Joinville, Prince de, 91
Joppa, Battle of, 14
Julius Cæsar, 5, 7, 9, 11

KATHARINE of Arragon, 8, 70
Knee-caps, 22, 29, 35, 36, 42, 52, 66, 85
Kolman, Desiderius (armourer), 98

LAMBESPRING, BARTHOLOMEW (goldsmith), 55
Lancaster, Earl of (Edmund Crouchback), 36, 42
Lances, 44-46, 74
Langford, William, 34
Le Botiler, 24
Lee, Sir Henry, 82, 85, 86
Leicester, Earl of, 81, 86
Lewes, Battle of, 22
Lincoln, Battle of, 14, 15
Littlebury effigy, 36
Long-bows, 75
Lothian, Lord, 90
Louis XI., 49, 59, 62
Lucas, Mr. Seymour, 65

MADRID armoury, 98
Magnus Barefoot, 12
Mail armour, 9, 12, 13, 16, 18, 22, 24, 27, 29, 45-47
Mantling, 32
March, Earl of, 42
Matthew de Paris, 24
Maule, Peter de, 24
Maximilian, The Emperor, 58, 66, 70, 73, 74
Melsa, Sir John de, 33
Men-at-arms, 43, 46, 47
Mentonière, The, 65, 92
Meyrick, 6, 65, 73
Milan, 82
Milanese armour, 52, 81
Missaglias, The (armourers), 52, 56, 69
Montfort, Simon de, 24
Montlhéry, Battle of, 47, 75
Monstrelet, 36

Morat, Battle of, 76
Morlems, 78, 92
Musée d'Artillerie, 34

NATIONAL Portrait Gallery, 22
Neck-guard, The, 52
Nottingham, Siege of, 14
Noyon, Battle of, 24
Nuremberg, 81, 98

PARHAM Collection, 18, 19, 34, 56, 61
Partisan, The, 75, 76
Paton, Sir Noel, 30, 33, 56
Pauldron, The, 69, 85, 86
Peascod, The, 92
Pembridge, Sir R., 30
Pembroke, Earl of, 22, 85
Pennant, 81
Petticoat, The, 50, 69
Philip II., 78, 98
Pickering, William (armourer), 90
Pikes, 75, 76
Pistols, 78
Plastron-de-fer. See Breastplate
Plate armour, 21, 22, 28, 29, 45, 47, 50, 74
Pliny, 6
Poitiers, Battle of, 43, 46, 49
Portland, Duchess of, 81
Pouleynes, 36
Pourpoint, The, 16

QUATREMAYNE brass, The, 56
Queen Mary's Psalter, 39, 42

RAYNE Church, 65
Richard I., 10, 14-16, 20-22, 24
Robert of Normandy, 22

ST. GEORGE's Chapel, 61
St. Pol, Comte de, 49, 62
St. Stephen's Chapel, 42
Sallads, 33, 57-59, 61, 62, 75
Sandwich, effigy at, 40
Scale-armour, 21
Scandinavians, The, 9, 22
Schloss Ambras, 82, 86
Seusenhofer, Conrad (armourer), 66, 70
Seusenhofer, Jörg (armourer), 82
Shields, 6, 19, 44
Shirland, Sir Robert de, 15
Shoulder-pieces, 39, 50, 52, 66
Shrewsbury, Battle of, 49
Sollerets, 36, 51, 56, 66, 69, 70, 90
Somerset, Duke of, 60
Sommers, Will, 73
South Kensington Museum, 65, 81, 82, 96
Spitzer Sale, 82, 85, 96
Spurs, 24, 39, 51
Staff-weapons, 75-77

Stafford, Sir Humphrey, 51
Standard, Battle of the, 14
Standard of mail, The, 47
Stephen, King, 16
Stevyns, Thomas (armourer), 55
Stothard, C. A., 22, 39, 40
Strutt, 12, 81
Sulney, De (brass), 36
Surcoats, 27, 35, 39, 40, 42, 46, 48
Sussex, Earl of, 85
Sword, Charles I.'s, 96
Sword, James I.'s, 96
Sword, John Hampden's, 96
Swords, 10, 85, 96-98
Swords, Legendary, 10, 11

TABARD, The, 48
Tacitus, 7, 8, 12
Tancred, 10
Tapul, The, 69, 85, 92
Tassets, 48, 50, 69, 85, 91, 92
Temple Church, The, 22
Topf, Jacob (armourer), 82, 86
Tower, The, 18, 20, 33, 66, 75, 76, 85, 86, 95, 96
Tuilles, 50, 51, 52, 66

VALENCE, AYMER DE, 36, 39, 42
Vantail, The, 20
Vence, 81
Vere, De, 23
Verneuil, Battle of, 47
Vinosse, 9
Vinsauf, 21
Viterbo, Battle of, 49
Visor, The, 32-34, 46, 56-60, 65, 66, 82

WACE, 15
Wallace Collection, 33, 86, 96
Wallace, William, 17
Waller, J. G., 19
Warwick Castle Collection, 18, 34, 36, 48, 73
Warwick, Earl of, 17, 51-55, 56, 66
Weaver, 39
Westminster Abbey, 36, 48, 61
Westmoreland, Earl of, 40
Whatton effigy, The, 40
William the Conqueror, 12, 20
William Longespée, 19, 22, 23
William the Outlaw, 16
William of Toulouse, 30
Wilton House, 85
Windsor Collection, 81, 90, 91, 92, 95, 96
Windsor Tournament, The, 29, 39
Woolwich Collection, 18, 33, 56, 61, 96
Worcester, Earl of, 85

ZOUCHE, Lord, 56

Printed by R. & R. CLARK, LIMITED, *Edinburgh.*

PART II
FOREIGN ARMOUR IN ENGLAND

LIST OF ILLUSTRATIONS

COLOURED PLATES

		PAGE
I.	Painted Wooden Shield of the fifteenth century. British Museum	Frontispiece
II.	A Marauder of the "Bandes de Picardie." Mr. J. F. Sullivan	14
III.	Half Suit, engraved and parcel-gilt. Duke of Westminster	24
IV.	Gold Damascening on russet ground. Late Italian suit. Tower of London	30
V.	Breast-plate, embossed and parcel-gilt. French. Mr. David Currie	38
VI.	Casque of an Officer of the Guard of Cosmo de' Medici. Mr. David Currie	44
VII.	Lower part of enriched Chanfron. Suit of Charles I. when prince. Tower of London	72
VIII.	Two Wheel-locks. German and French. Of the seventeenth century. Major Farquharson	84

ILLUSTRATIONS IN THE TEXT

1. Mail Hauberk from Sinigaglia. Sir Noël Paton's Collection . . . 19
2. Standard Collar of Mail. Royal Artillery Institution . . . 21
3. Gothic Armour. Said to be from the Church of Irene at Constantinople. At Parham 26
4, 5. Gothic Armour. Said to be from an old mansion in the Tyrol. Front and Back views. Sir Noël Paton's Collection 27
6. Gothic Armour. Probably Italian. Sir Noël Paton's Collection . 29
7. St. Michael. By Perugino. National Gallery 31
8. The Battle of Sant' Egidio. By Uccello. National Gallery . . 33
9. Carved Relief from the Visconti Tomb in the Certosa at Pavia. South Kensington Museum 35
10. German late Gothic Suit. Collection of Mr. Morgan Williams . . 42
11. Suit of Maximilian Fluted Armour. Belonging to Mr. Percy Macquoid . 43
12. Maximilian Armour from Eaton Hall. In the possession of the Duke of Westminster, K.G. 45
13. Engraved Maximilian Breast-plate. Burges Collection in the British Museum 46
14. Portrait. By Piero di Cosimo. National Gallery 47

LIST OF ILLUSTRATIONS

	PAGE
15. Helmet. Presented by Maximilian to Henry VIII. Tower of London	48
16. Cap-à-pie Suit of Henry VIII., on a Horse barded with Embossed Burgundian Armour of the time of Henry VII. Tower of London	49
17. Tilting Helm. Time of Henry VII. Westminster Abbey	51
18. Tilting Helmet. Early sixteenth century. At Penshurst	52
19. Tilting Helmet of an Ancestor of Sir Philip Sidney. Penshurst	52
20. The Sword of Battle Abbey. Fifteenth century. Collection of Sir Noël Paton	54
21. Sword of the Fourteenth Century with Guard for the Forefinger. Windsor Castle	54
22. German Armour. Date about 1570. The Duke of Westminster, K.G.	57
23. Suit of late Italian Armour. Embossed and damascened. Tower of London	61
24. Fine Italian Breast-plate, c. 1550. Said to have been worn by Philip of Spain. Collection of Mr. David Currie	63
25. Pair of fine Italian Gauntlets. Possibly belonging to the same Suit as the Breast-plate. Collection of Mr. David Currie	64
26. Embossed Gorget. French, c. 1550. Collection of Mr. David Currie	65
27. Silver Armour of Charles II. when prince. Tower of London	67
28. Sixteenth century Armet of rare form, with double visor. Mr. E. Cozens Smith	68
29. Suit of parcel-gilt Armour. Made for Charles I. when prince. Tower of London	69
30. Richly Embossed and Damascened Target. Italian, sixteenth century. Mr. David Currie's Collection	71
31. Target of Etched Steel. Italian or German, about 1550. Mr. P. Davidson's Collection	73
32. Roundel, with National Badges and Inscription. Belonging to Lord Kenyon	74
33. Hilt of Two-handed Sword with the Bear and Ragged Staff on the Pommel and Quillons in chased steel. Penshurst	75
34. Venetian Cinquedea, engraved, with Ivory Handle. The Duke of Norfolk	77
35. Main-Gauche with Steel Hilt. Belonging to Mr. Percy Macquoid	78
36. Main-Gauche with Silver Guard. Windsor Castle	79
37. Rapier with Silver Guard. Windsor Castle	79
38. Inlaid Ivory Cross-bow. Tower of London	81
39. Pistol by Lazarino Cominazzo. Collection of Major Farquharson	87
40. Early German Wheel-lock Pistol, used by the Reiters. Collection of Major Farquharson	87
41. Richly Decorated Flint-lock. Probably Spanish. Collection of Major Farquharson	91
42. Snap-hance of Italian make, about 1640. Collection of Major Farquharson	91
43, 44. Highland Pistols. Collection of Major Farquharson	92

PLATE I.—Painted Wooden Shield of the Fifteenth Century.
Burges Collection, British Museum.

FOREIGN ARMOUR IN ENGLAND

I

INTRODUCTORY

A FORMER monograph, *Armour in England*, treated of weapons and armour made either in this country or connected historically with English wearers. The more extensive field of foreign armour brought into England by wealthy and enthusiastic collectors is now embraced.

The enthusiasm felt for armour is not surprising; its interest is so many-sided. Not only are collectors fascinated by it, but students of history, artists, and antiquaries. As mere decoration it appeals to some, and finds a place in their abodes; but it is among artistic people that its more ardent admirers are found. Hence it is far from rare to find the glint of arms and weapons lighting up the artist's walls.

From the artistic standpoint nothing can be more picturesque than the varied forms assumed by armour and weapons in obedience to the all-powerful dictates of self-preservation, or to the more arbitrary changes of fashion. To realise what these changes mean, to appropriate them to the scenes and episodes of history, belongs to the painter, sculptor, and scenic artist. If anything in art should be accurately portrayed, it is the men and the events which make up history. Historic painting and sculpture, which might live long in art, may be disregarded by posterity owing to the anachronisms due to neglect of this important study. Most of the changes were perhaps efforts to avert the recurrence of some accident in the lists or field of battle. To definitely track them to their actual origin, to seek out the causes for the singular and ceaseless modifications arms and armour have undergone, is, however, work only possible to the antiquary. It is his province to open the door to the artist.

The quality of the art lavished as decoration on the gala suits of princes and nobles is superb. In mediæval days it was the prerogative of the male sex, the fighting sex, to deck itself like a game bird in gorgeous plumage; women's raiment was more subdued. To the male, no richness of dress that ingenuity could invent or wealth procure was denied. In preparation for those stately festivals when the courtier was to shine in the presence of the fair sex, his sovereign, and his peers, nothing was spared. The armour of parade intended for royal jousts and tournaments is as sumptuous as the wit of man could devise, with time and money unstinted. Chasing, embossing, engraving, damascening, and gilding of the most exquisite quality were lavished upon it, the designs, and possibly the actual work, being by the best artists of the day. The later suits, when cap-à-pie armour was mainly consecrated to festivals and little regarded in battle, were especially loaded with decoration. Besides its excellence of design and richness of ornament, the mere craftsmanship of the armour itself is of a quality that never can be excelled, and the modern counterfeiter, with all his skill and appliances, is baffled in the reproduction of *tours-de-force*, such as the high-combed morions of Italy and Spain.

To study the evolution of armour is like observing the works of nature. Necessity, it is well known, is the great stimulator of the inventive faculty of man, and no necessity is more cogent than that of self-preservation. In the long trials of skill, in which for generation after generation the armourer was pitted against the guilds concerned in the production of lethal weapons, the means of defence seemed once or twice so entirely perfected as to defy the weapons of the assailants. But ere long, the attacking forces, gathering energy, calling on the ingenuity of bowyers, fletchers, sword- and gun-smiths, seem again to emerge triumphant, armed with yet more deadly and powerful weapons. The struggle on the one hand to encase the man, like Achilles, in invulnerable armour, and on the other to break down his armour of proof, was like that between the gunners and naval architects to-day, but it lasted for centuries. It ended, as all such struggles must, in the complete discomfiture of the armourer; the increasing use and accuracy of firearms finally reducing defensive armour to a costly incumbrance. Nature, indeed, seems to will that all things, animate or inanimate, should succumb to persistent attack. Viewed in its true light, armour reveals all the stages, and is the very embodiment of, perhaps, the most prolonged and determined struggle that the development of civilisation has witnessed. It presents a gauge of the extent and limitation of man's inventive faculties, in other words, of his brain capacity, in the ages so-called mediæval.

Concerning the history of the vast bulk of the armour that falls into the possession of the collector, all is speculation, and its very nationality perhaps matter of conjecture. The place whence it has come is often purposely concealed by the dealer, and a legend concocted to invest it with a higher market value. The weapon may have played its part in the stern realities of war; the armour may have saved its owner, or, failing in the hour of need, contributed to the deaths of those who trusted to it. Little armour perished with the wearer. Next to gold and silver, the harvest of arms was the most coveted spoil of victory, and none remained ungleaned on the battle-field. What harvests such holocausts as Flodden Field must have presented, affording opportunities of refitting to the man-at-arms, archer, hobiler, billman, down to the rapacious camp-follower. Though etiquette may have hindered the squire of low degree from donning the full cap-à-pie armour of the knight he overcame, no doubt many a captor of rich armour sacrificed life to indulgence in the dangerous vanity of dressing beyond his station.

The historic and personal associations connected with the arms and weapons present at, and by whose agency were enacted, the decisive battles, the most stirring incidents of history humanity can witness, are not the least of the many-sided interests of armour.

Though but a small proportion of the vast number of suits, helmets, and weapons that have come down to us can be assigned to definite wearers, and most of even these were but the parade suits of royalty and the court, the few pieces of real actual fighting armour identified with particular owners are invested with extraordinary interest. Most of these owe their preservation to the ancient and poetic custom of hanging the arms of knightly personages over their tombs, a custom linked with the still older dedication of arms and armour at the obsequies of the dead, either by placing them in the grave or hanging them in the temples of the gods. The reality of the connection between the pagan and Christian customs is apparent by such incidents as that of William of Toulouse, early in the thirteenth century, who dedicated his helm, shield, and weapons to St. Julian, hanging them over his shrine; or that of the King of France, who, after the battle of Cassel in 1327, presented his victorious arms to the neighbouring church. The churches in fact ought to have been the great treasure-houses for actual armour, as they are of representations of armour on monuments and brasses. Unfortunately, however, the old veneration for the person of the dead which led to the consecration of the armour and weapons he had actually used, hardly survived the close of the thirteenth century. Cupidity induced the prelate to claim them as a perquisite of the burial function, as when the Prior of Westminster received £100 as ransom for the horse and accoutrements of John of Eltham; while the temptation natural to the survivor to retain the finely tempered weapons and armour, whose quality had been tested in the field, had always to be reckoned with. This reluctance to sacrifice them is beautifully expressed in such ancient ballads as those on the death of King Arthur.

Armour was moreover specially devised by will to be kept as heirlooms. Grose in the *Antiquities* states that Thomas Beauchamp, Earl of Warwick in the time of Henry IV., left to his son Richard by will the sword and coat of mail said to belong to the celebrated Guy, Earl of Warwick, he having received them as an heir-loom from his father. Sir Thomas Poynings, in 1369, devised to his heir the helmet and armour which his father devised to him. It also became penal to make away with armour. Enactments, such as that of 1270, commanded that all armour was to be viewed and kept in safe keeping under good security not to be let go, for the king's use at reasonable valuation. The custom, which prevailed extensively, of leaving the undertaker to provide property helmets and arms in place of those the departed had himself used, also tended to lessen the interest of even the arms which yet remain. That the helmet of Henry V. was provided by the undertaker is well known, and that he continued to provide arms down to Elizabeth's time, is shown by accounts of funerals such as of Lord Grey de Wilton in 1562, when among the items of the undertaker's bill are a "cote of arms," banner and bannerolles, a "helmett of stele gylt with fyne golde," with a crest gilt and coloured, a "swerde with the hyltes, pomell, chape, buckle, and pendant, likewise gylte, with a gurdle and sheathe of velvet." This custom of substituting spurious insignia at the solemn interment of the dead was set by the Church, who consigned mock croziers and chalices of no intrinsic value to the graves of even the most exalted prelates. But of the true and the spurious armour alike, time, rust, and above all, changes of religious sentiment in regard to the churches, have spared little besides an occasional helmet. The claims of neighbouring magnates, to the custody of what they regard as family relics, the temptation to sell, and lack of interest, have further sadly reduced this residue within the present century.

Yet neglect and depredations notwithstanding, the preservation of nearly all the English fighting helms known, from the time of the Black Prince to that of Henry VIII., and of many swords of early date, is due to their having been deposited in churches. Other magnificent fourteenth and even thirteenth century swords owe their preservation to their inclusion in the insignia of Municipal Corporations. Lincoln, Bristol, Kingston on Hull, Newcastle-on-Tyne, Southampton, Gloucester, Hereford, Exeter, Chester, Coventry, are among the cities still possessing these interesting relics.

If our national collections are less imposing than those of Spain, Austria, Italy, France, and Germany, the enthusiasm of wealthy amateurs has made this country second to none in the richness of its private collections of European arms and armour.

Of collections commenced and handed down from the time that armour was still in use, by far the most important is the Tower Armoury. Its history can be gathered from Lord Dillon's paper in the fifty-first volume of *Archæologia*, "Arms and Armour at Westminster, the Tower, and Greenwich." The collection had its origin in Henry VIII.'s passion for arms and armour, which was ministered to by Continental sovereigns, especially Maximilian, who shared this taste, and with whom he maintained a close friendship. His extensive array of tilting and jousting suits was kept at Greenwich, and an inventory taken of them upon his death. They were not removed to the Tower until perhaps 1644, though the armoury there was already, during the reign of Henry, one of the sights of London. The arms stored at Westminster were probably removed to the Tower as early as the beginning of the reign of Edward VI. The armoury was no doubt regarded more as an arsenal for use, than in the light of a collection, and perhaps was drawn upon constantly until the Civil Wars, when it was extensively depleted. Five of the Greenwich complete suits of Henry VIII. still exist, however, three mounted upon barded horses, as well as other pieces. The collection becoming on its removal a national one, several suits of distinguished nobles of Elizabeth's reign, and some of the royal armour of the Stuarts, were added. During the present century attempts to render it more complete have been made, by purchasing examples of enriched foreign armour, and more especially of pieces illustrating the armour of more ancient days. Many of the latter, however, are now pronounced to be spurious, and none of them are remarkable.

It appears that the Tower collection has been drawn upon, at some comparatively recent period, for the decoration of Windsor Castle. Some half-dozen of the richest suits are now in the Guard Chamber. Arrayed in cases in the north corridor is a most extensive collection of magnificent weapons, many intimately connected with the history of the country, as well as a matchless collection of oriental arms and armour, formed to a large extent from the collection at Carlton House and added to by Her Majesty.

The Museum of Artillery in the Rotunda at Woolwich contains a valuable collection of armour and weapons, formed partly from the Tower collection, and by judicious purchases. The series of Gothic armour from Rhodes is very remarkable. There are also a few pieces in the Royal Artillery Institution not far distant, and a small part of the collection has been placed in Dover Castle.

The British Museum contains a limited but choice collection, chiefly bequeathed by Mr. Burges, of Mediæval and Renaissance armour, as well as its unrivalled series of antique arms and weapons.

The South Kensington Museum also possesses a few interesting arms and weapons, besides collections deposited on loan.

The munificent bequest of the Wallace Collection has put the nation in possession of a superb series of armour only rivalled by that in the

Tower Armoury. It must unfortunately remain inaccessible, being packed away in cases until the rearrangement of Manchester House is completed; consequently none of its contents could be illustrated. It contains perhaps over 1200 specimens, without counting the Oriental arms, all of them choice and some unsurpassed. It is rich in Gothic, fluted, and highly decorated armour, and comprises a matchless series of swords and other weapons. Of private collections in this country that are historic, the Earl of Warwick's is undoubtedly the most interesting, part of it having been in the Castle from the days when armour was in constant use. Besides the few almost legendary pieces, it claims to contain armour of Lord Brooke, killed at Lichfield, of Montrose, the target of the Pretender, and Cromwell's helmet.

Among the armour at Wilton House are the superb suits of the Dukes of Montmorency and Bourbon, captured by the Earl of Pembroke at the battle of St. Quentin, together with the suit worn by the Earl, and pictured in the Jacobe Album. With these are a good number of lancers' demi-suits marked with the family initial. The armour of the Earl of Cumberland, also figured in the Jacobe Album, yet remains in perfect preservation in the possession of Lord Hothfield. The collection at Penshurst Castle comprises some good armour, including helmets and weapons of the Sidneys, its former owners. Sir Wheatman Pearson possesses the barded suit of fluted armour said to have been worn by a Talbot of Shrewsbury at the Field of the Cloth of Gold. Many other ancient seats still contain family armour, either relics of the Civil Wars, as at Littlecote and Farleigh Castle, or removed from the neighbouring church, or discovered in some attic, vault, or even well, as at Arundel.

The Armourers and Braziers Company possess one of the Jacobe suits in their small collection; the Benchers of the Middle Temple own some armour; and there are a few pieces in the United Service Museum in Whitehall. Mr. Leonard Brassey possesses a fine historic cap-à-pie suit of the hereditary challengers, the Dymoke family. Some of the Corporation Museums, especially at Edinburgh, comprise examples of armour and weapons.

It is unfortunate that nearly all the notable private collections made within the present century have been dispersed, either on the death of their owners, or before. The Walpole, Bernal, Meyrick, Londesborough,

Shrewsbury, Coutts-Lindsay, Brett, De Cosson, and many other collections have been scattered far and wide under the hammer. The Warwick and others have suffered severely by fire; and of collections made by the past generation probably only that of Lord Zouche at Parham remains intact.

A great deal of armour is absorbed as decoration, not only in such stately homes of the nobility as Arundel, Eaton Hall, Hatfield, Knebworth, but in private houses. Armour is also hidden away in small and unknown collections, like two in the writer's family, which would well repay careful examination. But undoubtedly the richest treasures are in the collections of wealthy amateurs, like Mr. David Currie, Sir Noël Paton, and above all in those of members of the Kernoozer's Club. It is impossible to convey, in a slight sketch, any adequate idea of the wealth of armour in the country, the real extent of which is as yet only to be surmised; but in spite of sales it is doubtless increasing yearly.

The fact cannot be ignored that, of all this mass of armour, very little has been made in England. By far the larger part was indeed certainly made in Germany, a country devoted to metal-working from the earliest periods of its history.

The first dawning of anything like European reputation for the production of arms and armour, since the collapse of the Roman Empire, was achieved by Germany. Owing to its political constitution, and perhaps extent and population, its towns were more enterprising in mediæval ages than ours, and acquired a name for particular manufactures at a relatively early period. The necessity the trading towns were under of arming their citizens to defend their freedom and privileges, amidst the semi-independent princelings and nobles who kept armed retainers and combined to levy blackmail, induced many to take up the manufacture of arms in self-defence, for which they afterwards sought a market among neighbours and abroad. In the thirteenth century, when St. Louis bore a German sword to the Crusades, the names of Cologne, Passau, Heilbronn appear almost simultaneously as seats famous for the production of lethal weapons. Cologne soon assumed the ascendency, at least in English eyes, for its weapons are spoken of with respect in many an early ballad. Thus the battle of Otterbourne is fought "with swords of fyne Collayne," and King Arthur's sword hails from Cologne :—

> For all of Coleyne was the blayde
> And all the hilte of precious stone.

The Duke of Norfolk having sent for armour out of Germany proves that its armour was already regarded as of superior excellence in the time of Richard II. German armour might have been used more largely in England and at an earlier period, but for want of sympathy, perhaps inherited from the Crusades. These, which knitted so many of the races of Europe into close contact, happened not to promote any *camaraderie* between Germany and ourselves. Their Crusades were undertaken independently, or were ill-timed relatively to ours. The unfortunate differences between Richard and the Archduke of Austria, which drained our country of so much gold and silver that even the chalices were melted, rendered Germany unpopular, and the feeling was not improved by the further great loss of treasure on the abortive election of Richard of Cornwall as Emperor. Princely intermarriages were unable to effect a union of hearts, for the Kings of Almayne never come out well in contemporary poetry. Nor was the perpetual presence of enterprising Hansa merchants in factories, such as the London Steleyard, calculated to promote good feeling, though introducing a large bulk of German goods into the country. Steel, itself a German word, was certainly amongst the imports, probably not only as a raw product, but manufactured into articles such as the "Colleyne clowystes" and "Cullen cleavers," and possibly sometimes defensive armour as well. Until late in the fifteenth century, however, the differences between the military equipment of Germany and England is more marked than between that of England and France, which country with the Netherlands formed a natural barrier that only strong common interests would effectively bridge. When bonds of trade began to knit peoples together, German armour, from its excellent quality, divided the market of the world with Italy. The accession of Henry VIII. opened the English market wide to it, his ambition to again dismember France, his alliance with Maximilian and relationship to Charles V. leading to distinct *rapprochements*. Natural inclination and political necessity strongly biassed him in favour of his wife's kinsmen, until his unhappy divorce left him isolated.

Italy vied with Germany in the production of armour, Milan taking the lead. Matthew of Paris heard, in 1237, from a credible Italian that Milan and its dependencies could turn out 6000 men on iron-clad horses. An item in the inventory of Louis Hutin, 1316, is "2 haubergeons de Lombardi"; and that of Humphrey de Bohun, in 1322, mentions Bologna "un haubergeon qu'est apele Bolioun." Italian armourers were established in Paris as early as 1332. Ancient British ballads abound in references to Myllan and Myllen steel. The Earl of Derby, afterwards Henry IV., sent to procure armour from Sir Galeas, Duke of Milan, and when he had selected all he wished for in plated and mail armour, the Lord of Milan ordered four of the best armourers in Milan to accompany the knight to England. In the fifteenth century Milan was able, after the battle of Macado in 1427, to furnish within a few days 4000 suits of armour for cavalry and 2000 for infantry. At a great Spanish tournament held in 1434, only Italian armour and weapons were permitted. Louis XI. and the Duke of Burgundy settled Italian armourers in their dominions. This king seized in 1481 a heavy convoy of cuirasses, sallads, etc., packed in cotton to prevent them rattling and imitating bales of silk, on the way to the Duke of Brittany, giving them to John Doyac as a reward for their discovery. Monstrelet mentions that the Milanese gave corselets and other armour to the Swiss, with the finest promises, before the battle of Marignano. Henry VIII. kept 1000 Myllen swords for the tourney in the Tower, and sent to Milan to purchase 5000 suits of "almain rivets." The most eloquent testimony to the excellence of Milanese arms is, however, to be found in the pages of Brantôme, a very keen observer on all matters military. Milan furnished the finest-engraved and most elegant corselets for *hommes de pieds* "tant de M. de Strozzi que de Brissac." "Ce genre de cuirasse legère eut la plus grande vogue à la cour de France"; and "on y approuvoit fort les corselets gravés de Milan et ne trouvoit point que nos armoriers parvinssent à la mesme perfection, non plus qu'aux morions." Strozzi, insisting that his armaments should be Milanese, "pria voire quasy contraignit tous ses capitaines de n'avoir plus autres armes, tant harquebuses, fourniments, que corselets de Milan" : while Guise wished his infantry to be armed not with muskets, but good harquebuzes de Milan—"de bonne trampe pour ne crever." Milanese armourers, like the Gambertis, were enticed to Paris ; Pompée a Milanese was selected to

PLATE II.—A Marauder of the "Bandes de Picardie."
In the possession of Mr. J. F. Sullivan.

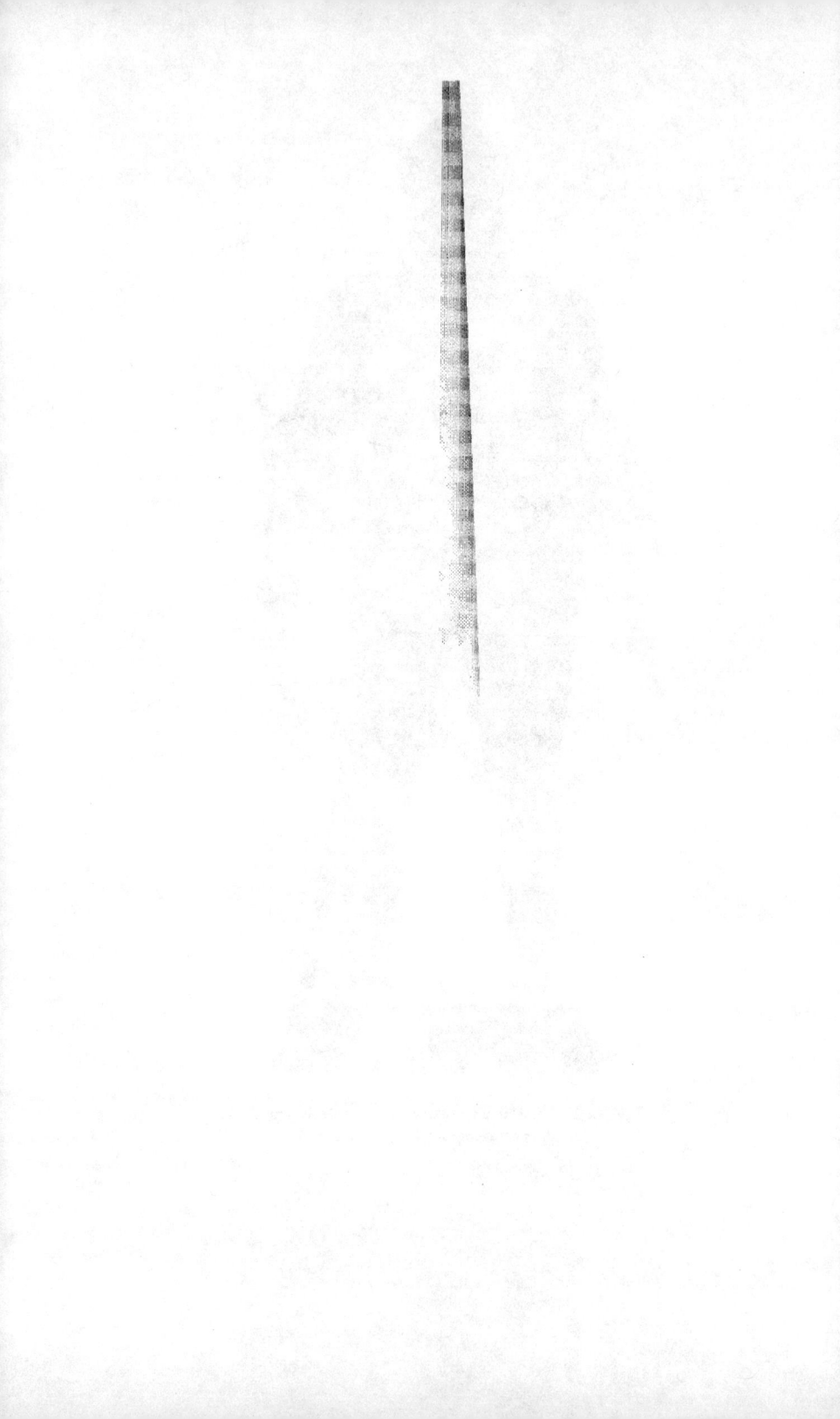

teach the King fencing, and Maistre Gaspar de Milan is pronounced "le meilleur forgeur qui jamais eut." Brantôme further describes the troops on their way to relieve Malta, "portant sa belle harquebuze et son beau fourniment de Milan," and adds, "car nous avions passé par Milan, où nous nous estions accommodez d'habillements et d'armes si superbement qu'on ne scavait pour quelz nous prendre, ou pour gentilshommes, soldats, ou pour princes, tant nous foisoit beau veoir."

Florence became later a great rival of Milan, and we find Wolsey negotiating with a Florentine for "2000 complete harness of Almayne rivettes at 16s. per set." Brescia was famed for its steel, and probably supplied the vast requirements of Venice, whose arsenals contained, in the seventeenth century, arms for 800,000 combatants. Henry VIII. requested permission from the Doge of Venice, in 1544, to purchase 1500 Brescian harquebuses, and over 1000 suits of horse and foot-armour. Pisa, Lucca, Mantua, Verona, Pistoja also produced armour and weapons of high quality.

Spain, with the most abundant and accessible supplies of the finest iron ores in the world, celebrated for its weapons from the time of the Punic wars, and with the immeasurable advantage of commanding the services of the Moorish steel-workers who were masters of the armourer's craft, ought to have maintained the first rank as armourers of the world. It probably did for centuries supply its own requirements. We find the Spanish warrior under James of Arragon, 1230, sheathed horse and man in mail, with his quilted *perpunto* or pourpoint beneath, and the iron *gonio* or breast-plate above; the iron greaves and shoes, helmet and shield. Thus equipped, the Christian rode down the Moslem by superior weight of man, horse, and arms, the Moors dispensing with pourpoint and breast-plate, and riding unarmoured horses. The helmets were of Zaragossa steel, and James's "very good sword, lucky to those who handled it," was from Monzon and called Tizo, as the more celebrated sword of the Cid was called Tizona. The most dreaded weapon, however, at this time, was the windlass cross-bow, whose bearers were mounted and carried large shields.

Little of the Moorish armourer's work has come down, though they worked steel extensively in Toledo and Seville. No Hispano-moresque swords exist of earlier date than the fifteenth century, and these have richly-worked hilts in the Arab taste. A few Moorish helmets are preserved, also of the fifteenth century, two of which, attributed to Boabdil, are in the Madrid armoury, and are also richly decorated in the Arab manner. The fame of Moorish armour is preserved in the words Morion and Morris pike. The famed swords of Toledo did not obtain renown until the Renaissance, and were not produced after the seventeenth century. Real Spanish armour appears very clumsy, and probably little, if any, was made much after the accession of Charles V. One of the latest suits in the armoury at Madrid is late Gothic in feeling, with a tilting helm of Henry VII., and marked with the poinçon of the city of Valencia.

France is very much in the same position as England in regard to armour, for no city in it ever established any permanent reputation as a seat of manufacture. Louis X. had a Toulouse sword—Louis Hutin's inventory comprises mail from Chambly. Metz, Pignerol, Abbeville are mentioned by Brantôme as producing armour inferior to Italian. Froissart speaks repeatedly of the excellence of Bordeaux weapons, but at the time when Bordeaux was English. The same is true of the Limoges steel. But Paris must after all have been the metropolis of French armourers. The description by Froissart of the battle of Rosebecque, fought in 1382, where the hammering on the helmets of the combatants made a noise that could not have been exceeded if all the armourers of Paris and Brussels had been there working at their trade, shows that these cities were great centres for the production of armour. The names of very few French armourers have escaped oblivion, however; and Italian workmen were employed in France from at least the time of Louis XI. Some beautifully decorated French armour exists, chiefly early seventeenth century, but in France, as in England, most of the armour was probably obtained from Italy and Germany, when once the superiority of their work was definitely established.

Netherlandish armour was always in high repute, and some of the Brussels armourers achieved European fame. It even set the fashion, as we read that Sir Gilbert Talbot, 1353, provided himself with "a curas complete of Flanderis makyng of the new turn for £20." Very few specimens that can be identified as Belgian or Flemish exist, however, in collections.

II

CHAIN MAIL

THE immense antiquity of chain mail, and that it originated in the East, are the two facts beyond dispute in its history. Its fine-linked structure exposes, however, the maximum surface of the perishable iron to atmospheric decay, and hence few specimens of great antiquity are known. The two shapeless masses of iron rust in the British Museum, brought from Nineveh by Layard, only reveal on close examination that they were once supple and glittering coats of mail. Whether these are to be assigned to the Nineveh of Sennacherib or to the Sassanian period, they equally claim to be the oldest actual relics of chain mail in existence. The jackets sculptured on the Trajan column are unusually faithful and realistic renderings of chain-mail armour, for the labour and difficulty of an exact reproduction of the minute and complicated repetitions of form into which the links of mail group themselves are generally evaded by a variety of conventional ways of expressing its texture.

The wearers of mail were nomadic horse—Persian, Parthian, and Scythian, and inhabited a belt stretching obliquely from the Caspian in the direction of Scandinavia, the mysterious and imperfectly known amber trade perhaps keeping these peoples in touch. The Viking became acquainted with mail and brought a knowledge of it to Western Europe; his descendants wore it in their expeditions to the East, completing the circle when the mail-clad Crusaders under Cœur de Lion met the mail-clad horse in alliance with the Saracens on the plains of Ascalon. Coats of Eastern mail called gasigans, as told by Geoffrey de Vinsauf, formed part of the spoils of victory taken by Richard, especially on the capture of the great caravan near Galatin in 1192.

Although an immense quantity of mail exists in collections at home and abroad, it can as yet neither be dated nor located upon its intrinsic structure. The links of the Viking suits discovered in the peat morasses of Denmark are as carefully formed as those from Persia or India of the present century. The fashion of the garment is the only guide, but whether the mail is of the period of the garment, or older material made up, cannot be determined. It continued to be used in the West until the seventeenth century, and to a much later time in Eastern Europe; and it is probable that no scrap of such a costly material was ever discarded. It was not passed on and absorbed by foot soldiers, who seem rarely to have cared to use it.

The Norman hauberk did not open down the front, but was drawn over the head by the attendants just before the engagement commenced. Wace relates that Duke William's mail was drawn on wrong side in front in sight of the English. The Norman Duke is the only person represented with leggings of mail in the Bayeux tapestry, and to the absence of these Harold's death and the fate of the day were directly due. His first wound was the turning-point of the battle, twenty Norman knights breaking in and securing the standard. An armed man, says Wace, struck him on the ventaille of the helmet and beat him to the ground, and as he sought to recover himself a knight beat him down again, cutting him on the thick of the thigh to the bone. Girth and Leofwine fell in this onset. The manner of a death which sealed the fate of England must have made a deep impression on the victors, and thenceforth mail chausses became an essential part of the knight's equipment. That any genuine specimens of either the sleeveless or the long-sleeved hauberks of the eleventh or twelfth or even the thirteenth century have been handed down, is improbable. Many mail suits, however, have been acquired in the belief that they were European, and of great antiquity, to the disappointment of their owners, like those adorning the Hall of the Middle Temple, which are modern Persian. One of the oldest, perhaps, is that said to have been found in making a road in Phœnix Park in 1876, and alluded to in *Armour in England*. The oft-repeated statement that it was found associated with a silver badge of the O'Neills has been ascertained by Mr. T. H. Longfield, F.S.A., to be baseless, the badge having been purloined from the ancient harp in Trinity College, Dublin, on which it is now replaced. The hauberk, now in the writer's possession, is of large size and reaches to the middle of the thighs, with short sleeves, and is exquisitely made. Mail shirts, sleeves, etc., of later date than the

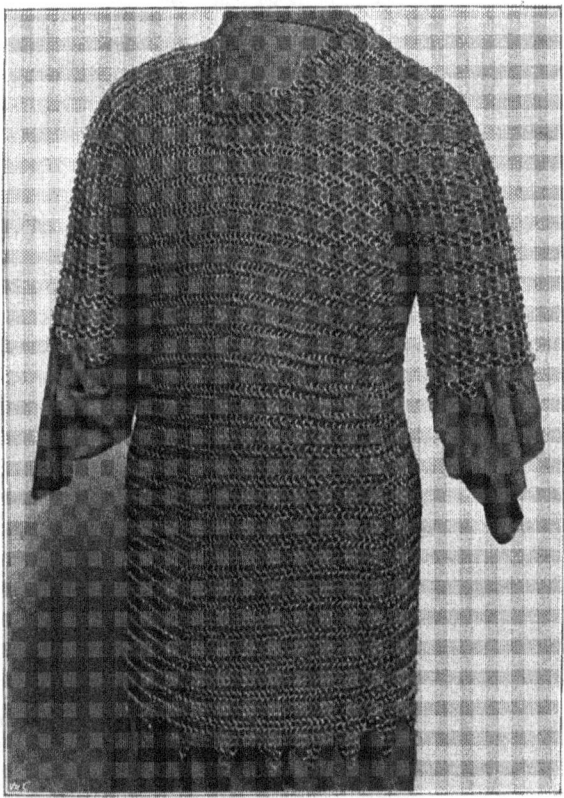

FIG. 1.—*Mail hauberk from Sinigaglia. Sir Noël Paton's Collection.*

fourteenth century are far from uncommon, and are represented in every collection. By the kindness of Sir Noël Paton a most perfect fourteenth century specimen is illustrated. It is close fitting, and was exhibited in 1880, and described by Burgess as " one of the few coats of mail which have any decided history." In Meyrick's *Critical Enquiry* we are told that "it had been purchased by a Jew from an ancient family at Sinigaglia, near Bologna, in whose possession it had been beyond any of their records." A note further informs us that "the Jew bought it by the ounce and paid for it forty guineas." Sir Samuel Meyrick observes that it corresponds to the coat of mail on the statue of Bernabo Visconti at Milan. It may be described as a single coat of mail with no slits and no reinforcement. It measures 2 feet 9 inches from the top of the collar, and has sleeves which are 10 inches long from the armpit. " It is wider at the bottom than at the waist, two gussets being inserted for this purpose. The rings average a good half-inch in their interior diameter ; half are riveted and half are continuous, the latter have a pear-like section, the rounded parts being on the inside circumference. The riveted rings appear to have been made of circular wire, but have become rather flattened, probably by wear. The rivets are of the pyramid shape, like those of the Dublin coat of mail, but much bolder and larger. There is a row of brass rings round the neck, and the bottom of the edge and sleeves are finished by vandykes, also in brass rings, riveted with iron. This is probably the finest coat of mail that has come down to us." One of the figures guarding the Maximilian cenotaph wears a precisely similar hauberk. Italian pictures in the National Gallery show that the custom of finishing off mail defences with several rows of brass links, to form some sort of scolloped edging, was universal in Italy during the fifteenth and sixteenth centuries. French and English monuments and manuscripts prove that this custom extended to Western Europe, the scolloped edge commonly showing over the tassets from beneath the pourpoint.

Vestiges of the camail are found on fourteenth century bassinets just as they are seen in the conical helmets from Nineveh and on the Trajan column. The standing collar or gorget superseded it. Fig. 2 reproduces a perfect specimen belonging to the Royal Artillery Institution at Woolwich, of exquisite work, with the links round the throat reinforced or doubled. Though gorgets of plate were introduced as early as 1330, many still preferred to wear the mail, so that they continued more or less in use for two centuries longer. Mail was generally worn bright. In the fourteenth century *Anturs of Arthur* we read :

His mayles were mylke quyte, enclawet full clene
His stede trappet with that ilke, as true men me told.

An early fourteenth century stanza, the 39th of the "Armynge of King Arthur," suggests that the surcoat over mail was to keep off rain and not sun. The colour green was almost universally used from the reign of King John.

With scharfe weppun and schene
Gay gownes of grene
To hold theyr armour clene
And werre it from the wette.

For a brief period in the sixteenth century, mail was again worn

Fig. 2.—*Standard Collar of Mail. Royal Artillery Institution.*

without plate armour. The custom was revived in Italy when assassination was rife, and is seen in portraits of Italian noblemen in the National Gallery.

The costume of the unfortunate Wyatt on his rebellion is described in the chronicles of Jane and Queen Mary as "a shert of mayll with sleves, very fayre and thereon a velvet cassoke and an yellowe lace with the windelesse of his dag hanging thereon, and a paire of botes and spurres on his legges; on his hedd he had a faire hat of velvet with broade bonne-work lace about it." Soon after a "shippe laden with shertes of mayll" was brought in by Strangwyshe the Rover, "who came from the French king and submitted to the Queen's mercy." The celebrated duel between Jarnac and La Chateigneraye was fought in shirts of mail.

In the Scottish wars of Edward I. it was a common saying that "arrows can penetrate the hardest mail"; and more efficient armour had to be devised. Simon de Montfort, standing like a tower and wielding his sword with both hands, was pierced in the back by a foot soldier who lifted up his mail. The hero died with "Dieu merci" on his lips; not the only victim who met his death in this manner. The change in the fashion of armour was hastened by such events. The process has already been traced: it began at the knee-caps, which were covered by plates called poleyns. Three actual and perfectly unique specimens of these, belonging to Sir Noël Paton, show that they were not laid upon or over the mail, but replaced it, as represented in monumental effigies. One pair with parallel sides is finely embossed and vandyked, closely resembling those of some early fourteenth century effigies. A globose example formed of three articulated plates is still more interesting, having been richly damascened with an arabesque design worked in thin brass lines, the field being delicately and closely cross-hatched with incised lines. The really remarkable and unexpected surface decoration this discloses explains the nature, and confirms the accuracy, of certain fourteenth century representations of black armour covered with fine gold arabesques. The cross-hatching served to retain the black pigment, and gave a dark cast to the steel surface, enhancing the value of the delicate brass inlay.

The process of reinforcing the mail defence was continued, as we have seen, until it was entirely cased with an outer shell of plate. A quilted coat was worn beneath the mail, if not a second one between the mail and plate armour. These multiplied defences must have made active fighting difficult and most fatiguing, and were discarded so soon as a light armour of fine steely quality, and without crevices, was procurable.

III

GOTHIC ARMOUR

PLATE armour reached the perfection of workmanship in the second half of the fifteenth century. At no period was it so light, yet impervious, with curves and angles so admirably directed to deflect the impact of sword or lance, and articulations so skilfully devised to mitigate the restraint on freedom of movement necessarily imposed by a sheathing of steel. Never was armour so closely fitted to the contour of the body, and thus so elegant, so easily and therefore so constantly worn. This, the so-called "Gothic Armour," is the cynosure of collectors, and is so rarely to be obtained that a fairly perfect cap-à-pie suit may command some £2000.

This Gothic armour is the armour of the Van Eycks and Memling, of Perugino and Leonardo, and of the earlier works of Albert Dürer. The sumptuously illuminated French and English manuscripts of the fifteenth century depict it in use in every vicissitude of war or combat, by sea and land, on horse and foot, and testify how little it impeded the freedom of action of the wearer. They show that it was rarely concealed in campaigning by any textile garment, and also that when worn by prince or noble, it might be gilded, entirely or partially, even almost fantastically. Thus the upper half may be gilt, and the nether limbs left burnished steel; or these gilt and the body steel; but more often the alternate plates of the articulated breast and back defences, the arms, or the elbow and knee pieces, are gilt, while the rest presents the normal sheeny surface of steel.

The general characteristics of Gothic armour have been described in *Armour in England*, illustrated in Fig. 19, by the fine and accurately modelled suit of the Beauchamp effigy at Warwick. Though many fine suits have been brought to this country from abroad, none are in any way connected with English wearers, and none could therefore be illustrated in the former monograph. It seems incredible that nothing should have been preserved either of the weapons or armour with which the long struggle for supremacy in France was maintained during the minority and rule of a king, too studious and placable for days when his turbulent subjects cared only for war. Of the armour and weapons of the thousands of men-at-arms who fell victims to the Wars of the Roses, the direct outcome of the disappointing issue of the French Wars, and so annihilating to English art, perhaps but a helmet and a few weapons remain. The extermination of the old nobility; the completeness of the change in habit and thought introduced into this country by the Renaissance, affecting alike art, literature, and costume; the change in religion, the revolution in the science of warfare, and the absolute centralisation of the ambitious and luxurious nobility in the court or camp of Henry VIII., together with that vainglorious and wealthy despot's passion for extravagant dress, novelty and pomp, combined to break most effectually with the past and to render all Gothic armour mere obsolete lumber. Contemporary pictures of Henry VIII.'s proceedings, especially of his meeting with Maximilian, in which the English retinue is equipped in the new closed armet while Germans wear the old visored sallad, as well as the accounts of his forces and his purchases of arms, convince us that out-of-date armour and weapons, even if still serviceable, were no longer, as heretofore, passed on to the lower ranks of retainers. Hall relates of the muster of the city bands in the thirty-first year of Henry VIII. that "all were put aside who had Jackes, coates of plate, coates of mail, and bryganders, and appointed none but such as had whyte harness, except such as should bear the morish pykes, which had no harness but skulles." The destruction of obsolete armour in this reign must have been very complete, for no suits of the Gothic armour worn down to this date by the fathers and grandfathers of the courtiers of Henry have been preserved.

France and the Low Countries have been swept nearly as bare, anything that might have been spared by former ages having been finally destroyed when the houses of the nobility were gutted during the

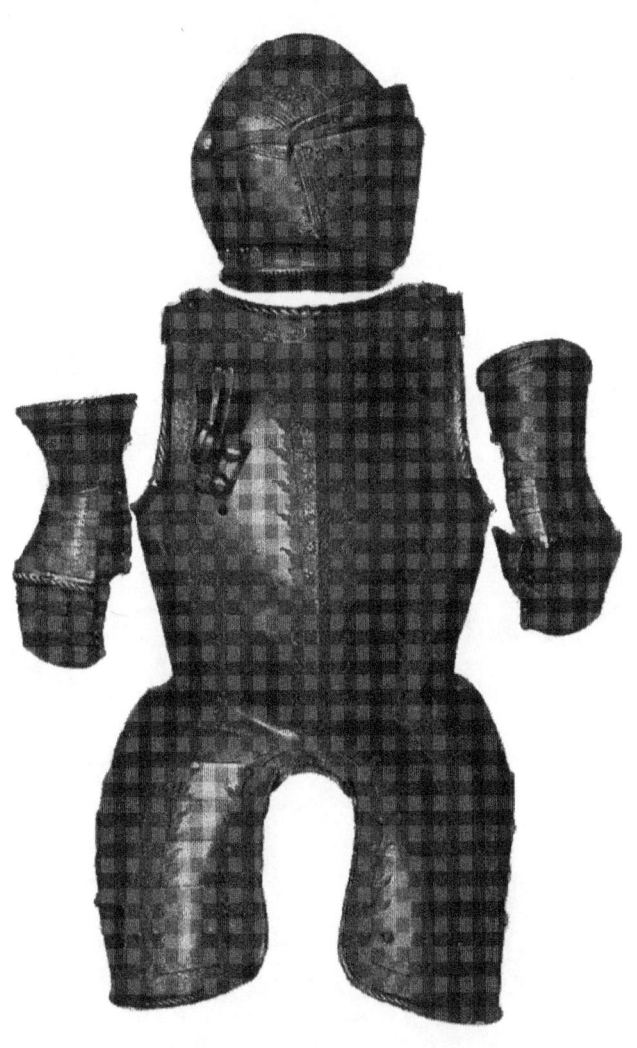

PLATE III.—Half Suit, engraved and parcel-gilt.
Collection of the Duke of Westminster.

Revolution. In more conservative Italy and Spain a few Gothic suits have escaped destruction, and though the Art Renaissance of the one, and wealth and pride of the other, were inimical to the preservation of obsolete arms, yet probably some few specimens have passed from the hands of private possessors into those of wealthy amateurs of France and England. Germany, however, has ever been the inexhaustible treasure-house whence Gothic arms and armour have leaked from the hands of private possessors into those of collectors. In Germany even the trading towns had clung to their ancient buildings, walls, and traditions, and in many of the old Town Halls the furniture, arms, and weapons of the civic guards, and the old implements of punishment and torture, are still preserved. The innumerable feudal castles of the lesser nobility have to a yet greater extent preserved the belongings of their ancient occupants, who clung to their titles, heraldry, arms, and weapons as symbols of vanishing rights and power, and of ancient pretensions and privileges, so out of harmony with the world beyond. The ubiquitous and assiduous dealer has long found in them a happy hunting-ground for arms and weapons, whence to obtain the bulk of those he disposed of.

In addition, some important stores of Gothic armour have been disgorged from the Levant, trophies of the incessant wars maintained by the Turks against Christendom. A large quantity existed at Constantinople, and the story goes that a ship, some fifty years ago, was actually freighted to Genoa with old armour as ballast. The indefatigable dealer Pratt of New Bond Street became possessed of some of this armour, which he made up into suits in the best way he could, restoring but too liberally the parts that were missing. The suit illustrated, Fig. 3, is in Lord Zouche's collection at Parham, where it is catalogued as from the Church of Irene at Constantinople : it no doubt formed part of this consignment. The head-piece, an Italian sallad, is of later date, while the remainder, though so beautiful in form, does not appear to be either entirely homogeneous or complete. Other suits in Lord Zouche's extensive collection are from the same source. Another much smaller series of Gothic armour was brought to England from the Isle of Rhodes and most fortunately did not pass through the hands of any dealer, and is thus in an absolutely trustworthy condition, the very rust not having been removed. It consists of a number of pieces, approximately of one date, many of particular elegance and interest, both on account of the armourer's marks, and the examples of engraving they present.

FIG. 3.—*Gothic Armour, said to be from the Church of Irene at Constantinople. At Parham.*

By the kindness of Sir Noël Paton two of his four fine Gothic cap-à-pie suits are illustrated. The first, Figs. 4 and 5, is German work of the second half of the fourteenth century.

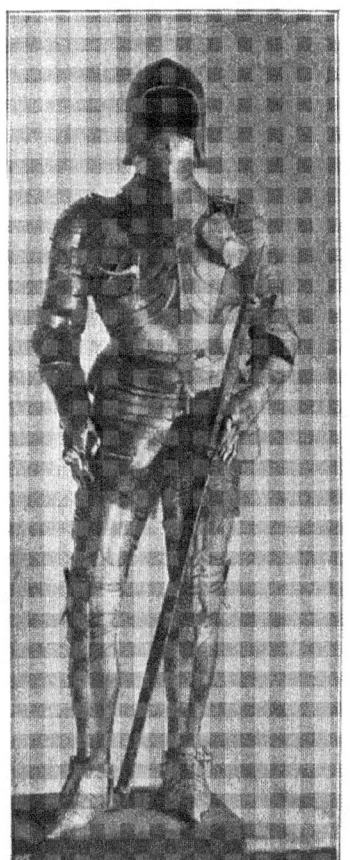 

FIGS. 4 AND 5.—*Gothic Armour. Said to be from an old mansion in the Tyrol. Front and Back views. Sir Noël Paton's Collection.*

Sir Noël observes that "the upper part of the suit especially is remarkable for its perfect condition, the original straps being intact, and the inner and outer surface of the metal having been scarcely touched by rust." The graceful and doubly articulated and engrailed breast and back-plates are beautifully designed, and finished in the manner of the great master armourer Lorenz Colman of Augsburg. The curiously plain collar is attached to the pectoral by a bolt and staple, and there is a fixed lance-rest, these appliances adapting the suit for tilting rather than war. There are no tuilles, one of the most persistent features of Gothic suits, and no pauldrons or shoulder-guards. The brassards, coudières, genouillières, formed of an unusual number of plates, and especially the gauntlets, are of great beauty, and resemble those of Lorenz Colman's suits. These and the *solerets à la poulaine retroussé*, to quote Sir Noël's description, " are exceptionally beautiful and artistic in design. Of the sollerets, however, unfortunately only the left, with its fine long-necked spur silvered and thickly patinated, is genuine." " The head-piece is a strong bassinet of the type styled barbute by Viollet le Duc, and possibly of somewhat earlier date, and bears on either side the armourer's mark." The fine preservation of the metal " is due no doubt to the fact that the suit had remained for many generations in one place—an old mansion in the northern Tyrol, whence so late as 1872 or 1873 it was obtained by a well-known Parisian dealer, from whom it passed to Pratt of New Bond Street ; after whose death it came into my hands."

The second of Sir Noël's suits (Fig. 6), of about the same date, resembles more the armour of Italian pictures and actual Italian suits. The articulated and channelled breast-plate is remarkably bold and graceful in its lines, as are the entire brassards, more especially the coudières. "The spiked rondelles and the gauntlets have much picturesque character, and the tuilles are exceptionally fine in form. The sollerets are of the kind called *arc tiers point*. The head-piece is a close helmet of good design and apparently contemporary. In general effect the armour is light but dignified : though the breast-plate bears a Gothic R, no history attaches to it.

The great interest and beauty of the Parham suit, Fig. 3, lies in the particularly elegant and finely laminated and engrailed breast and back-plates. Like Sir Noël's German suit, it has no tuilles and retains the staple for fastening the collar and the lance-rest. The sollerets and perhaps some other pieces are restorations. It is without armourer's marks, but resembles Nuremberg work in general form and detail.

Two magnificent Nuremberg Gothic cap-à-pie suits are in the Wallace Collection, at present inaccessible. One is on foot, partly fluted, consisting

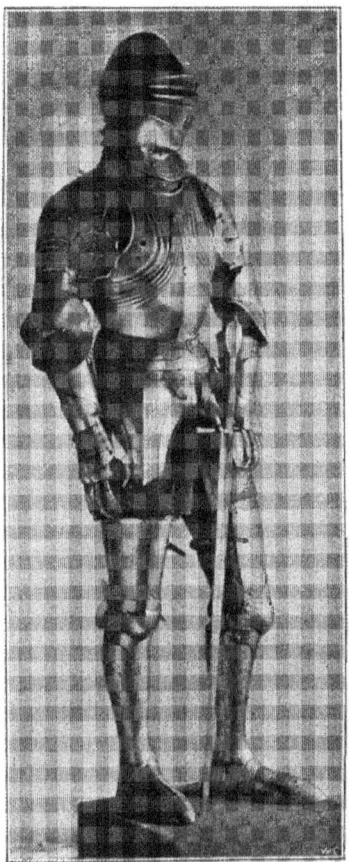

FIG. 6.—*Gothic Armour. Probably Italian.
Sir Noël Paton's Collection.*

of sallad with movable visor, mentonnière, jointed breast and back-plate, and quite complete body armour with pointed-toed sollerettes, and skirt of riveted mail. The other, for man and horse, is equally complete and ornamented with brass bands, the sallad with visor and mentonnière being of fine form and contemporary.

For suits of Gothic armour which have belonged to known wearers, and have been handed down with unbroken pedigree, we must go to the great collections of Europe, and especially to those which, like the Viennese, were commenced while armour was still worn. Of sculptured representations of Gothic armour none surpass the Beauchamp effigy at Warwick. A no less accurate figure is that by Peter Vischer, also in gilt bronze, of Count Otto IV. of Henneburg, 1490, from the Church of Romhild in Thuringia. There is a cast of this in the South Kensington Museum, as well as one of the gilt bronze effigy of Count Weinsberg at Munich, in armour which is remarkable in several respects. Italian Gothic armour of different periods can best be studied in the National Gallery. A suit (Fig. 7) of about the close of the century is from one of the compartments of the famous altar-piece by Perugino, removed from the Certosa at Pavia in 1786, and painted according to Vasari about 1490. It represents St. Michael in full armour, except the head. The underlying mail shows, as usual in Italian pictures, at the elbows, the skirt, and below the knees, and has a deep edging of brass rings. The breast-plate, though in two, is arranged so that the body could not easily be bent. The shoulder-guards are less exaggerated than in contemporary French and English armour, but the elbow-guards seem large, angular, and loosely fitting. The sollerets are well made, unpointed, and leave the red stocking exposed at the toe and heel. The sword, on the left hip, is in a velvet scabbard with a beautifully and simply worked steel hilt and cross quillons slightly curved towards the blade. The shield is fine in form and typically Italian, bearing a Medusa's head and other classic ornaments, boldly embossed. The hands are bare, the right holding a slender staff or wand. In the figure of St. William by Ercole di Giulio Cesare Grandi of Ferrara, the head is bare and there are no plate defences to the neck, shoulders, or forearms. The top of the mail shirt shows as a narrow band round the throat, and covers the shoulders with short and very wide-open sleeves, its lower edge appearing between the tuilles over a second skirt of mail. Mail appears again below the knees and forms the covering of the feet, all edges being finished with rings of brass as usual. The breast-plate is

PLATE IV.—Gold damascening on russet ground. Late Italian suit. Tower of London.

large, plain, and of one piece; there are but three taces, with bold, finely formed, and ridged tuilles. The brassards, including the large butterfly-shaped coudière, appear from beneath the widely open sleeves of mail.

FIG. 7.—*St. Michael. By Perugino. National Gallery.*

The leg armour is also plain, but with the wings of the genouillières exceptionally large. The sword, unsheathed, is a magnificent weapon with gilt or brass pommel and grip and horizontally curved quillons. The striking figure of St. George by Pisano, in the broad-brimmed Tuscan hat, is of earlier date, as the artist died in 1451 or 1452. The mail shows beneath a thick quilted surcoat over which the great ill-fitting shoulder and other body defences are fixed. The limbs are almost completely sheathed in plate over the mail, but the pieces fit so loosely that the whole has a shambling appearance and seems ready to fall off. The sollerets are square-toed with long rowelled spurs. The armour represented in Boccacino's Procession to Calvary is almost identical, save that the mail sleeves are less baggy and shoulder pieces are worn. The St. William in Garofalo's Madonna and Child from Ferrara, though probably painted in the 16th century, preserves the exaggerated butterfly wings to the coudières and genouillières, and the Gothic tuilles, but has fluted sollerets and shows no mail. The St. Demetrius of L'Ortolano, who painted in the first quarter of the sixteenth century, shows fluted shoulder pieces and coudières, and half sollerets, leaving the front of the foot to a defence of mail.

The most interesting picture in the National Gallery (Fig. 8) to the student of armour, however, is that representing the battle of Sant' Egidio by Uccello, fought in 1416, when Carlo Malatesta, Lord of Rimini, and his nephew Galeazzo, were taken prisoners by Braccio di Montone. Uccello was born in 1397 and died in 1475, but there is no evidence as to the year in which the picture was painted. It appears to represent an attempt to rescue the Lord of Rimini, by a knight clothed cap-à-pie in very advanced plate armour and wielding a horseman's hammer. The breast and back plates are articulated; tuilles, where worn, are very short; the large pauldrons are of very varied construction, and either roundels or coudières with butterfly expansions are worn indifferently; in all cases the figures are completely cased in plate armour, though some wear mail gorgets, except that Malatesta has been partly disarmed and is protected by mail alone. De Commines observes that it was the law of arms in Italy to strip those taken to their shirts and dismiss them. The chief interest lies in the head-pieces, which, except in the cases of the prisoners and some trumpeters, are closed armets with baviers and visors hinged at the side, of varied form, the occularia being in all cases notched out at the upper margin of the visor and forming either round or half-round holes or slits. These armets are provided with most fantastic crests and plumes, the crown of the helmet being in several cases covered with

Fig. 8.—*The Battle of Sant' Egidio. By Uccello. National Gallery.*

velvet, overlaid with goldsmith's work and merging into the crest. All have the roundels at the back of the neck.

Another notable representation of an Italian battle (Fig. 9), in which the mounted combatants are clothed in complete typical Gothic armour, is

Fig. 9.—*Carved Relief for the Visconti Tomb in the Certosa at Pavia. South Kensington Museum.*

to be seen in the cast from the Visconti Tomb of the Certosa, Pavia, in the South Kensington Museum. The armour is of the most beautiful type, and the figures are singularly supple and full of action. The armet is more fully developed and almost uniform in type. The visor works on pivots, the occularium is a slit above it, and the bavier is a separate piece fastened by straps at the back. The event represented is the battle before Brescia in 1402. As a full-sized representation of the latest Italian Gothic armour nothing can perhaps be finer than the fifteenth century effigy of Guidarello Guidarelli surnamed Braccioforte from Ravenna, of which there is also a cast in the South Kensington Museum. The tuilles are flexible and pointed, formed of narrow horizontal plates; the shoulder-plates are bossed into lions' heads; and the armet has a double visor without bavier.

The statue of St. George, made by Donatello for the Florentine corporation of armourers in 1416, is almost Roman in costume and of little interest.

The account of the almost contemporary battle of Fornovo, 1495, by Philip de Commines bears testimony to the excellence of this Italian armour, especially of the close armets. The flower of the allied forces of Italy consisted of 2500 men-at-arms under the Marquis of Mantua, Count di Cajazzo, and Signor John Bentivoglio of Bologna, with other nobles, all well barded, with fine plumes of feathers and bourdonasses, or hollow lances, brightly painted, and used in tournaments. Great bodies of men-at-arms were in reserve. The French van contained 350 men-at-arms, 200 mounted crossbow-men of the king's guard—who fought on foot, however—300 archers and 3000 Swiss foot, several of the highest nobility dismounting to fight amongst them. In the main body were the king's guards, pensioners, 100 Scottish archers, about 900 men-at-arms, and 2500 Swiss, the whole army not exceeding 9000 men. The Italian men-at-arms delivered a charge, with lances couched, at a gentle gallop; the Estradiots, who should have supported them with their scimitars, retired to plunder the sumpter-horses; whereupon the men-at-arms who had charged and broken their lances fled, and their infantry gave ground. Those who had not charged also threw away their lances and fled, sword in hand, and were pursued and cut up. With the French were "a great number of grooms and servants, who flocked about the Italian men-at-arms, when they were dismounted, and knocked most of them on the head. The greatest part of them had their hatchets (which they cut their wood with) in their hands, and with them they broke up their head-pieces, and then knocked out their brains, otherwise they could not easily have killed them, they were so very well armed; and to be sure there were three or four of our men to attack one man-at-arms. The long swords also which our archers and servants wore did very good execution." The losses on the French side were but three gentlemen, nine Scottish archers, twenty horse of the vanguard, and some servants. The Italians lost 3500 men on the field, of whom 350 were men-at-arms, including six or eight of the Marquis of Mantua's relatives and other persons of quality. The lances "lay very thick upon the field, and especially the bourdonasses; but they were good for nothing, for they were hollow and light, and weighed no more than a javelin, yet they were finely painted."

Battles in England were much more serious affairs and were stubbornly contested. Those of the Wars of the Roses opened with a cannonade, after which the archers engaged and the billmen followed, nobles fighting on foot in their ranks to encourage them. Lord Richard Herbert "twice by fine force passed through the battaill of his adversaries," at Banbury, "polle axe in hand": at the battle of Towcester many were taken because they left their horses and decided to fight on foot. The Earl of Warwick dismounted at Barnet to "try the extremity of hand strokes"; but penetrating too far among the enemy to encourage his men, and not being properly supported, he was slain.

At Bosworth the archers formed the forward on both sides. Richard's archers " with a sodein clamour lette arrowes flee at theim. On the other syde they paied theim home manfully again with the same. But when they came nere together, they laied on valeauntly with swordes." The Earl of Oxford, however, kept his men in close order, and the enemy gave way, wholesale desertion sealing the fate of the battle. Henry was not engaged, but kept afar off "with a fewe companye of armed menne." Richard on horseback made a desperate attempt to get at him, but was unsupported and slain.

The English costume is described in the Plumpton Correspondence, when the Archbishop of York, having dues to collect in 1441, quartered 200 men-at-arms in Ripon and held it "like a towne of warre." These borderers wore breast-plate, vambrace, rerebrace, greves and guischers, gorgett and salett, long spears and lancegayes." English levies were not always so well armed. The 5000 men who came down from the north in the reign of Richard III. were "evell apparelled and worsse harneysed in rustic harneys." Under Henry VII. the Duke of Bedford took out " 3000 mene which were harneysed but barely, for theyr breste plates were for the most parte lether." The array taken to Calais by Edward IV. in 1475 is in striking contrast to this. Hall relates that " the men were so well armed and so surely in all things appoynted and provided that the Frenche nacio͡ were not onely amased to behold them, but much more praysed them and there order. In this army were 1500 men of armes well horsed, of the which the moste parte were barded and rychely trapped, after the most galiard fashion, havyng many horses decked in one suyte. There were farther 15,000 archers beryng bowes and arrowes, of the which a greate parte were on horsebacke. There were also a great number of fighting men and others, as well to set up Tentes and Pavillions, as to serve their Artilarie." De Commines adds that the men-at-arms, comprising the flower of the English nobility, were richly accoutred after the French fashion, well mounted, most of them barded, and each one with several persons in his retinue.

This Gothic armour, the lightest and most graceful ever produced, was ideal so long as it was customary for men-at-arms to fight indifferently on foot or mounted. The mixed tourney was still in vogue, fought the first day with sharp spears, the second day with swords, the third on foot with poll-axes. The Lord Scales and the Bastard of Burgundy, and the Duke of Albany and Duke of Orleans fought such tourneys, the latter having the misfortune to kill his antagonist by a spear-thrust. It was, in battle too, most honourable to fight on foot among the archers, and there was always a large number of gentlemen volunteering among them to "encourage the infantry" and make them fight the better. "The Burgundians had learnt this custom from the English when Duke Philip made war upon France during his youth for two-and-thirty years together without any truce." De Commines adds that at Montlhéry the order was given to the Burgundians that every man should alight without any exception. Knights equipped by the most renowned of the armourers of Italy and Germany were almost invulnerable until overthrown ; but English and Burgundian armour was not an equal protection, as the rash Duke of Burgundy, who seems to have had all his armour home-made at Dijon or Hesdin, discovered to his cost on the field of Nancy, when his

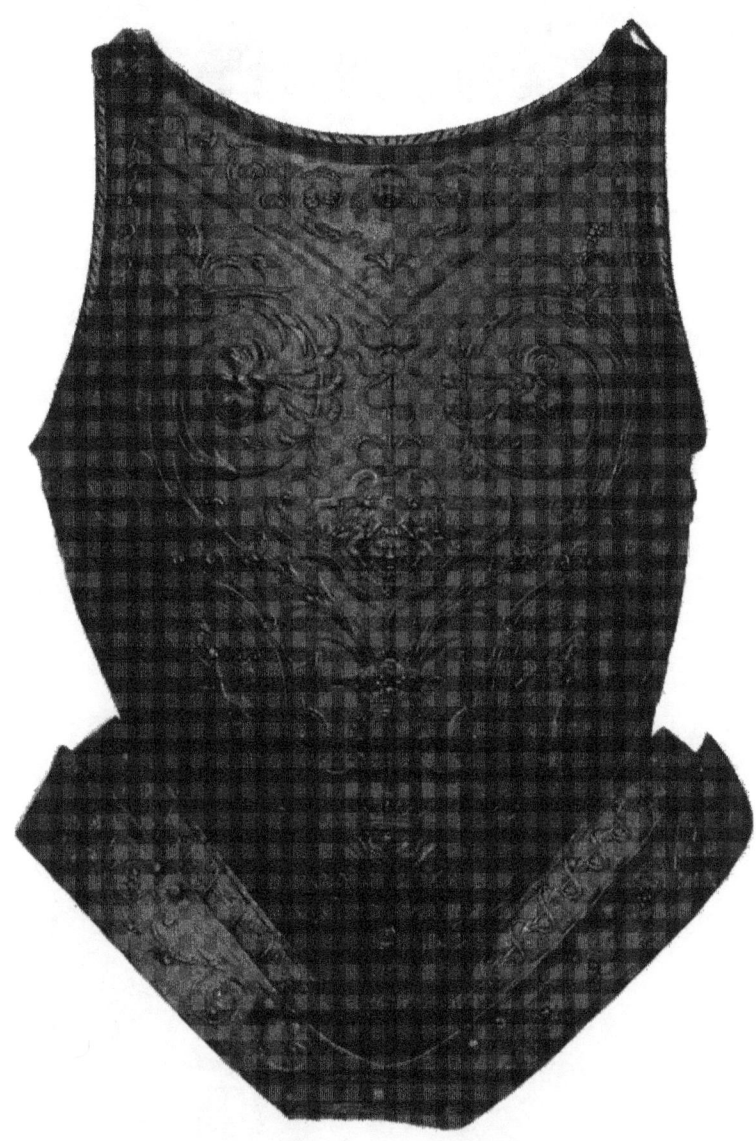

PLATE V.—Breastplate, embossed and parcel-gilt. French.
Collection of Mr. David Currie.

skull was cloven by a halberd, and two pike-thrusts penetrated the lower part of his body.

This fashion of armour appears to have been devised in the ateliers of the Missaglias of Milan. A work by Wendelin Böheim, custodian of the Imperial collections of armour in Vienna, published last year in Berlin (*Meister der Waffenschmiedekunst vom xiv bis im xviii Jahrhundert*), gives a short biographical sketch of this renowned family of armourers, who migrated to Milan towards the middle of the fourteenth century, from Ello, a village not distant from Asti and Lake Lecco. Petrajolo da Missaglia, the founder of the family, settled in Milan as an armourer towards the middle of the fourteenth century, and built the house in the Via degli Spadari where his sculptured poinçon or armourer's mark is still to be seen. The work of his son Tomaso da Missaglia greatly augmented the already world-wide reputation of the armour of Milan, and deserved in 1435 the recognition of Filipo Maria Visconti, who freed him in 1450 from taxes until his death somewhere about 1469. The armour by him is plain, the best known being that at Vienna of the Palsgrave Frederick the Victorious about 1450, with closed helm, roundels, unfingered gauntlets, and pointed sollerets over 13 inches in length. The suit is less graceful than German Gothic armour. The equally renowned son of Tomaso, Antonio, was born about 1430, assisting in his father's extensive business at the age of twenty. Large commissions were received, such as that in 1466, of the value of 20,000 lire, for 100 harness for the ducal mercenaries, and others from Duke Francesco, the Pope, Don Alfonso of Arragon, afterwards King of Naples, etc. On his father's death in 1469, their great patron the Duke presented him with an estate and mill, and in 1470 he added the iron mines near Canzo to his patrimony. Soon after, in 1492, a Venetian envoy sent home an account of Missaglia's works, finding finished harness to the value of many thousand ducats. His death took place near the end of the century; the exact date being unknown, like the name of his immediate successor. There are mentions of several Missaglias about whom little is known, one working in 1466 for Louis XI. Antonio was the last to bear the name of Missaglia, succeeding members of the family assuming that of Negroli, a name first met with about 1515, when a Giovanni Negroli appears as master of the works. The tomb in St. Satyro, Milan, preserves the inscription *Negroli da Ello qualunque detto Missaglia*. Few examples of Antonio's work are known. One of these, a plain suit made for the Neapolitan Count Cajazzo about 1480, is in the Vienna Imperial collections. The breast and back plates are not articulated, the pauldrons and tuilles are large and massive, coudières elegant, only the right gauntlet fingered, the leg-pieces with few articulations, and the suit, as so often seen in illustrations, is minus the sollerets. The head-piece is a sallad singularly painted in oils with the Count's armorial bearings, reminding us of the beautifully painted armour of Pisano's St. George published by the Arundel Society, which must have been executed prior to 1450. A jousting suit by him of much later date is engraved and partly gilded, apparently made in 1498 for an envoy of Ludovico Moro to the Emperor Maximilian.

Italian Gothic armour is very much rarer than German. Thoroughness is a German characteristic, and once embarked on a given course the German pursues it until, as is so apparent in their general iron-work, the result becomes exaggeration verging on the grotesque. The Missaglias introduced a certain grace of line into Milanese armour, and the German armourers pursued this vein, making the figures erect and slender and imbuing the waist and bust with womanly elegance. The Italians probably kept to much the same lines, for most representations of armour towards the third quarter of the fifteenth century display the same graceful characteristics, brought to a pitch, however, but little consonant with the stern realities of war, and brusquely set aside before the close of this century.

One of the most formidable of Missaglia's competitors north of the Alps was Hans Grünewalt, born about 1440 and died 1503, regarded by Böheim as one of the foremost armourers of his day. The founder of the bells of St. Sebaldus in 1396, Heinrich Grünewalt, appears to have been the grandfather of a family which became considerable in Nuremberg, building the still standing Pilatus House, properly the "Zum geharnischten Mann." Hans was employed by Maximilian when King of the Romans, and no armourer in Germany was more sought after. While he flourished Nuremberg was the most renowned of any city of Germany for the production of armour, but on his death Augsburg was allowed to entirely supplant it.

The Colman family migrated from Bâle to Augsburg about 1377, to again quote from Böheim. Georg, the father of Lorenz, was well established as an armourer when he was joined in 1467 by his famous son. In 1477 they were honoured with a commission from Maximilian, then King of the Romans, for a complete harness for horse and man, which was executed to his entire satisfaction. Georg died two years later. In 1490 Lorenz was appointed Court Armourer, and he had prospered so far as to be able to afford pecuniary assistance to the ever-needy Maximilian. Towards 1506 he worked for the Court of Mantua, receiving through the house of Fugger a payment of no less than 4000 florins for a harness which gave such satisfaction that a further sum was sent him as a present. In 1507 Maximilian again employed him, and in 1508 begged him to repair personally to Court, when probably the important change in the fashion of armour, resulting in the Maximilian fluted armour, was devised personally between Lorenz and himself. The first edition of Hans Burgkmair's woodcut engraving of the Emperor in a full suit of this armour for horse and man appeared in this same year. Lorenz died in 1516. The only authentic suits by him known to Böheim are in the Imperial collections of Vienna. One is the magnificent Gothic suit made in 1493 for Maximilian, a far more complete and defensive suit than those we have figured, but with similar fleur-de-lis pattern engrailing to the margins of the plates, while some of the upper edges on the limb pieces are rolled over and finished with a cable border. The suit is graceful and of exquisite workmanship, slightly fluted in the arms, with fingered gauntlets and moderately long and pointed sollerets. Three other tilting suits bear the Colman mark, the close-helmet surmounted by a cross, with the Augsburg badge and guild mark.

The Germans, however, as a race were not all lithe and supple men, and the burly high-living barons could not follow, and hence must have detested the elegancies of Gothic armour. They soon affected an opposite extreme, the clumsy sturdiness seen in so many of the portrait statues of the contemporaries of Maximilian round his cenotaph in Innsbrück. Fig. 10 represents a complete and characteristic suit of this kind belonging to Mr. Morgan Williams. It greatly resembles one figured by Böheim, made for Count Andreas von Sonnenberg about 1508, by Koloman Colman, and now in Vienna. Our suit, preserved in a Rhenish Castle, bears evidence, however, of being considerably earlier, and is regarded by its owner

as of about 1495. It is perfectly plain except for some slight fluting on
the mittened gauntlets, made to look as if fingered, and on the square-

Fig. 10.—*German late Gothic Suit. Collection of Mr. Morgan Williams.*

toed sollerets. The tuilles are still an important feature, but wide and plain.
Some German suits of this date look affectedly ungainly; such as a

mounted suit attributed to Duke John of Saxony, which is slightly fluted and bears the great tilting helm.

Fig. 11.—*Suit of Maximilian Fluted Armour. Belonging to Mr. Percy Macquoid.*

The Maximilian fluted armour is a development of this, belonging, however, rather to Renaissance than Gothic times. With its introduction the elegance so distinctive of late Gothic armour passed definitely out of fashion and gave place to armour in which the opposite characteristics were sought. The flutings which invest the Maximilian suits with so much character must have been suggested more or less by the shell-like ridgings and flutes of Gothic armour. The leading idea was the substitution of a stiff unyielding defence for one that was supple and pliable. The articulations of the breast and back plates—except in rare instances, such as the magnificent Nuremberg suit formerly worn by Lord Stafford, in which the breast-plate was formed of two pieces and decorated with graceful open-work tracery—were wholly abolished, and replaced by a stout and rigid pectoral more adapted to receive the shock of the lance in the tilt-yard. The form of tourney had changed, and was now chiefly tilting with a light and hollow lance, calculated to shiver at the impact, as may be seen in specimens still preserved in the Tower. The pliable Gothic suits adapted for mixed tourneys and for actual warfare were out of place in the tilt as now practised; and the heavy man-at-arms in full cap-à-pie armour had ceased to play the preponderating part in war and was shortly destined to disappear from the field. No longer was his function, as hitherto, to engage in the melée, and bear the brunt of the battle: this was sustained by the pike, arquebus, light-armed cavalry and artillery; the heavy-armed cavalry being reserved for charges in which the weight of man and horse sheathed in steel might ride down the opposing force.

All the cap-à-pie suits of fluted Maximilian armour resemble each other in their more salient characteristics. They are extremely defensive and well made, with every piece more or less fluted, except the greaves, which are usually perfectly plain. Many of the pieces have turned-over edges worked into cable patterns. The pauldrons and coudières are well developed, the gauntlets mittened, sollerets with very broad and square toes, breast-plate generally globose, but sometimes brought to a blunt point, often with a roundel guarding the left arm-pit. The armet has usually a low central cabled comb with parallel flutes on either side, occasionally there are three or five combs. The visor is usually thrown into three or four horizontal peaks or ridges, often with the underhung look believed to have been introduced in compliment to the House of Hapsburgh. An almost equally common form is the puffed visor, but

PLATE VI.—Casque of an Officer of the Guard of Cosmo de' Medici.
Collection of Mr. David Currie.

the form of the head-piece is generally more varied than that of the rest of the suit. The fine Nuremberg suit, Fig. 11, owned by Mr. Percy

Fig. 12. *Maximilian Armour from Eaton Hall.*
In the possession of the Duke of Westminster, K.G.

Macquoid, shows the bellows visor and the rope crest, and in it all the leading characteristics of Maximilian armour are well displayed, especially the duck-bill sollerets, the flutings of which boldly finish in ram's horns.

The suit formerly belonged to the King of Prussia, and seems to be perfect, except the collar, an apparent restoration.

Maximilian armour is greatly favoured by collectors. There are cap-à-pie and barded suits in the Tower and the Wallace collections, at Warwick, and in the collections of Mr. Panmure Gordon and Sir

FIG. 13.—*Engraved Maximilian Breast-plate. Burges Collection in the British Museum.*

Wheatman Pearson. The horse armour, which nearly entirely sheathes the head, neck, and fore- and hind-quarters, is fluted, gracefully curved, and except the crinière, worked in large pieces, the lower margins curving well away from the flanks. Three-quarter and half suits are well represented in the Tower and the Wallace collections, the one figured, Fig. 12, being a finely typical example brought from Strawberry Hill, and now the property of the Duke of Westminster. This armour seems to have been at times partly gilded, and instances exist where small badges are repeated to form bands of raised work between the flutes. It is sometimes engraved with borders of floral design, either edging the different

FIG. 14.—*Portrait. By Piero di Cosimo. National Gallery.*

pieces, or more boldly treated as in Fig. 13 from the Burges Collection in the British Museum. Though mainly worn in Germany, fluted armour became everywhere the fashion, the portrait by Piero di Cosimo, Fig. 14, in the National Gallery affording an admirable representation of a breast-plate with delicate flutes on the lower half. An actual specimen resembling this, but engraved, is in the collection from Rhodes at Woolwich. The corselets furnished to the Swiss pike-men by the Milanese appear also to have been of this pattern. Besides the bellows visor, and one puffed out to give breathing space and fluted, the visor was at times embossed into the form of a grotesque face with mustachios. Sometimes the helmets in which this occurs had a pair of fan-like appendages in pierced and fluted steel, forming a dignified and wing-like crest. The remarkable example in the Tower, Fig. 15, once silvered, and presented by Maximilian himself to Henry VIII., has a pair of ram's horns instead

FIG. 15.—*Helmet. Presented by Maximilian to Henry VIII. Tower of London.*

of wings. It has since been painted and rendered more absurd by spectacles, and assigned without any reason to the King's jester, Will Somers.

These grotesque helmets were sometimes worn with armour puffed and slashed to imitate civilian dress. A few pieces of this kind are in the Tower, but the Wallace Collection possesses a three-quarter suit, slashed, puffed, engraved, and gilt, the armet having the bellows visor and five-roped comb. The extreme of exaggeration to which German armourers were carried is seen in the suit in the Ambras Collection, figured by Hefner and by Hewett, in which the cloth bases as well as the puffed sleeves of the civilian are carefully imitated in steel. The

visor is singularly grotesque, and the whole presents a ludicrous and ungainly appearance, as well as being quite unserviceable.

The cap-à-pie suit of Henry VIII., Fig. 16, belongs to this group, and though not fluted, is made like the Maximilian armour, the high erect shoulder-piece and large coudières giving it a striking character. The armet is of fine form, with the visor thrown into the series of peaks and ridges common to fluted armour, and known to collectors as the bellows shape. The bridle-hand wears the mainfere (main-de-fer), while the right hand grasping the spear is gauntleted. The horse armour, though so boldly embossed, is of earlier date, not later than Henry VII. The

FIG. 17.—*Tilting Helm. Time of Henry VII. Westminster Abbey.*

foliated scrolls surround the *cross ragulé* and steel brickets and fire-stones, so that it probably presents a rare specimen of the Burgundian armourer's craft.

The head-piece for tilting used in Germany and England during the reign of Henry VII. and first years of Henry VIII., and known a century earlier, is represented, Fig. 17, by the remarkably perfect specimen found in the triforium of Westminster Abbey in 1869. It weighs 17½ lbs., the few others known in England weighing, with one exception, considerably over 20 lbs. When fixed, the helm itself was immovable, but as there were quite three inches of space round the head, movement inside was possible. The occularium is placed so that the head must be lowered to see out, the combatants sighting each other like bulls before making their rush, and throwing up the head to escape splinters of the lance.

The abandonment of this heavy helm for a much lighter form may have been due to Henry VIII. himself. Hall narrates that tilting on one occasion in 1524, with his great friend and brother-in-law Brandon, Duke of Suffolk, he had on a helmet of a new fashion, devised by himself, the like of which had not before been seen. It had a visor, which was up and unfastened, leaving the king's face exposed, when by some mischance the word was given to Brandon to start. No doubt in the old helm, and remarking that he could not see, he couched his lance, striking the king on the brow of the skull-piece or main portion of his helmet.

FIG. 18.—*Tilting Helmet. Early sixteenth century. At Penshurst.*   FIG. 19.—*Tilting Helmet of an Ancestor of Sir Philip Sidney. Penshurst.*

Appalled at the narrow escape, he vowed he would never tilt with his sovereign more. One of the lighter forms of tilting helmet, Fig. 18, from Penshurst, shows the small trap-door for speaking or breathing, but now riveted down. A second helmet, Fig. 19, of rather later date, is surmounted by the porcupine crest in wood, removed in the illustration, and is interesting as having belonged to the grandfather of Sir Philip Sidney. Both these helmets perhaps hung in Penshurst Church.

The sallad, the head-piece *par excellence* of Gothic armour, continued in use, especially in Germany, until far into the sixteenth century. In its simplest form it was the archer's head-piece: but provided with slits for vision, pulled over the brow in time of danger to meet the chin defence or bavier, it became almost a closed helmet; and with the further addition of a visor and other reinforcing pieces, it was used for battle or tilting by the mounted knight. It was never a very safe head-piece, De Commines relating how the Count of Charolois received a sword-wound on the neck at Montlhéry, 1465, for want of his bavier, "which, being slightly fastened in the morning, dropped from his head in the battle —I myself saw it fall." The Venetian form survived during the seventeenth century, though for pageantry rather than use, being covered with red velvet richly ornamented with beaten iron foliage and scrolls, gilded and sometimes surmounted by a swan-like crest. The richness of decoration of the sallad has been alluded to in the former monograph. The battle picture by Paolo Uccello, Fig. 8, shows one covered with red velvet and studded with nails. Elizabeth with her own hands garnished the sallad of Henry VII. with jewels, and in 1513 Erasmus Kirkener received £462 : 4 : 2 for "garnishing a salet" and a head-piece, "and mending a shapewe." Pope Pius V. sent Alva a sallad and sword for his brave fights for the Church. Wooden shields covered with painted canvas, embossed leather, or gesso, continued in use in Germany down to about the end of the reign of Maximilian. The magnificent specimen, Plate I., is now in the British Museum. Of late fifteenth century date, it is of wood lined with leather, faced with canvas, over which a layer of gesso has been laid to receive the gilding. Upon the gold ground the design has been painted, a knight in Gothic armour, with armet and poll-axe on the ground before him, kneeling to a lady, with the appropriate legend *Vous ou la mort*. The surfaces are finely curved. In the Tower inventory, quoted by Lord Dillon, among the jewels is a target of the Passion with Our Lady and St. George.

The splendid decoration of the sword-hilts used with Gothic armour has already been noticed. By the kindness of Sir Noël Paton an exquisite specimen in the finest preservation is illustrated in Fig. 20. The pommel and cross-hilt are plated with silver gilt, and the former bears a shield with the arms of Battle Abbey and the initials T. L. of Abbot Thomas de Lodelowe, 1417-1434. It came into the possession of Sir John Gage, K.G., on the suppression of the monasteries, his descendant presenting it to the Meyrick Collection. Few existing swords, except those used as municipal insignia, are in equal preservation, but richly worked hilts are represented in brasses and monuments. Swords

54   FOREIGN ARMOUR IN ENGLAND

abounded in churches, but few are left besides the royal swords at
Westminster, Canterbury, and Windsor. Part of the glamour surround-
ing Joan of Arc was due to the consecrated sword taken by her from St.
Catherine's Church at Tours. The sword of Guy, Earl of Warwick, was
specially mentioned in a will of the time of Henry IV., and its custody
confirmed to the family after the accession of Henry VIII. It is curious

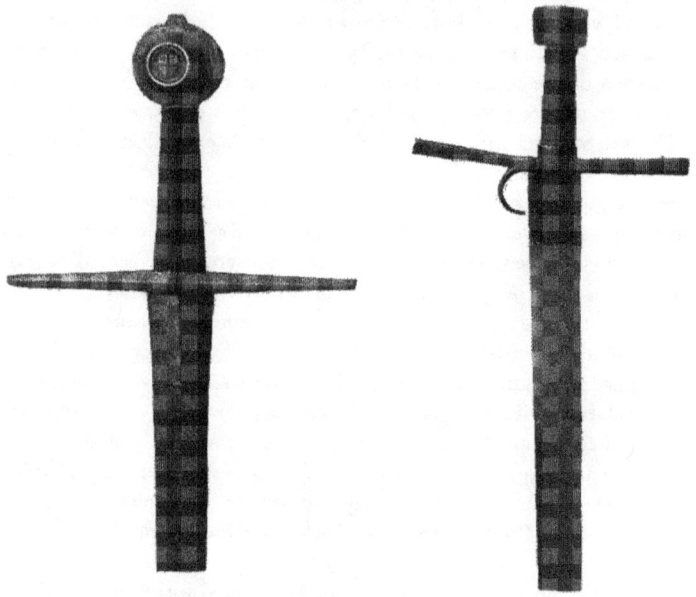

FIG. 20.—*The Sword of Battle Abbey.*   FIG. 21.—*Sword of 14th century, with*
Fifteenth century. Collection of Sir Noël Paton.   *Guard for Forefinger. Windsor Castle.*

to note that in 1319 the wearing of swords in London was forbidden, and
those confiscated were hung up beneath Ludgate, within and without.

The interesting sword, Fig. 21, from Her Majesty's collection at
Windsor, dates from about the end of the fourteenth or early in the
fifteenth century. Its peculiarity is the semicircular guard for the forefinger growing out of one of the quillons, the first step, as Baron de
Cosson remarks, " towards the evolution of the beautiful and complicated

rapier of the sixteenth century." "The pommel and guard are of iron fully gilt, the grip of wood." The blade is gilt and engraved for a few inches where it shows dark in the illustration, and is inscribed with the name of the Cid Marchio Rodericus Bivar and a shield of arms, these having been added, in the Baron's opinion, in the sixteenth or seventeenth century. Only four swords with the little semicircular guard or "half pas d'ane" were known when he described them, being introduced owing to the Italian custom of bending the forefinger round the quillon when slashing.

IV

ENRICHED ARMOUR

ARMOUR was enriched in almost all ages, sometimes ostentatiously so, and at other times left affectedly plain. It was, however, only when wearing it in battle ceased to be a paramount necessity, that armour definitely became little more than a mere vehicle for lavish display. Lightly armed and easily manœuvred troops and artillery were steadily becoming increasingly important factors in deciding the fortunes of battle, and at last men could with difficulty be brought to undergo the fatigue of carrying weighty armour which they regarded as no efficient protection. Sir James Smith's complaint in 1530 puts the matter clearly : " But that which is more strange, these our new fantasied men of warre doo despise and scorne our auncient arming of ourselves, both on horseback and on foot, saying that wee armed ourselves in times past with too much armour, or peeces of yron (as they terme it). And therefore their footmen piqueurs they do allow for very well armed when they weare their burgonets, their collars, their cuirasses, and their backs, without either pouldrons, vambraces, gauntlets, or tasses." This arming is even lighter than Mr. J. F. Sullivan's picturesque Marauder of Picardie (Plate II.). The Battle of the Spurs perhaps did much to break the prestige of men-at-arms, who were routed by one-tenth their number of English horse. The French chivalry, armed cap-à-pie, came on in three ranks thirty-six deep, and were targets as usual for the English archers, who lined a hedge, " and shotte apace and galled the French horse." The English horse, and a few mounted archers who had gone forward with spears, " set on freshly crying St. George," whereupon the French fled, throwing away " speres, swordes, and mases," and cutting the bards of their horses. The Estradiots

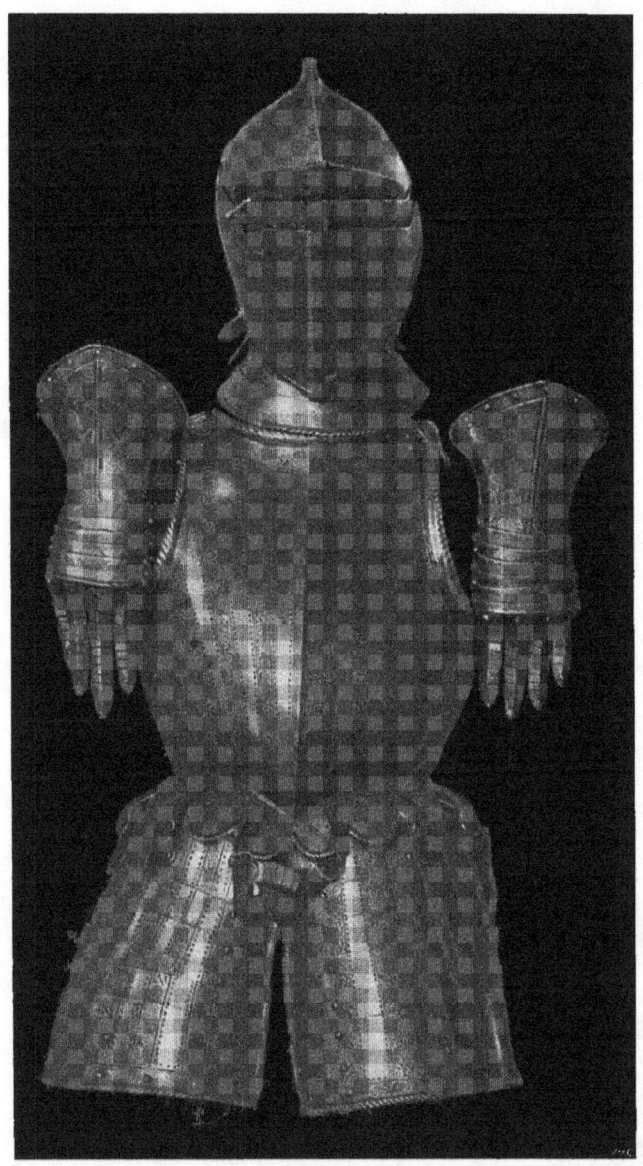

FIG. 22.—German Armour. Date about 1570. The Duke of Westminster, K.G.

coming down in front of the French host caught sight of the English horse, and mistaking the king's battaille of foot for horse also, turned and fled, chased by the Burgundians and Walloons; the main body of English, on foot with the king, having no opportunity of engaging.

The large proportion of mercenaries retained on either side contributed more perhaps than anything else to the disuse of armour. Nicander Nucius relates that in Henry VII.'s expedition to Scotland there were " Italians in no small number, and of Spaniards, and also moreover of Argives from Peloponnesus." In 1546 Lord Grey de Wilton brought his " Bullenoyes and Italian harquebuziers" from Boulogne. In invading Scotland two years later he divided " his menne of armes, demilaunces, and light horsemenne into troops, appointing the Spanish and Italian hagbutters on horsebacke to keepe on a wing." Captain Gambo, a Spaniard, and others held command, and, " being backed by the Almayne footmen, entered againe into Scotland."

In proceeding to quell the insurrection in Devonshire, Lord Grey's forces included, among other strangers, a band of horsemen " most part Albanoyses and Italians," and a band of Italian footmen under Captain Paule Baptist Spinola of Genoa. These mercenaries armed themselves in their own fashion and were not to be controlled. Nor does it appear that the Tudor kings were anxious to put even their body-guards in anything like complete armour. Henry VII.'s guard consisted " of fifty yeomen, tall personable men, good archers, and divers others." A little later, on the marriage of Prince Arthur, the guard consisted of 300 carrying halberts, in white and green damask, with garlands of vine embroidered back and front, richly spangled in front and enclosing a red rose worked in bullion and goldsmith's work. Nicander Nucius says that " they consisted of halberdmen and swordsmen who used bucklers and Italian swords, so that resting the bucklers on the ground, they could discharge arrows." Perkin Warbeck, posing as the " Whyte Rose Prince of England," had a guard of thirty in " Murray and blewe." Henry VIII. appointed a guard of fifty "speeres" in the first year of his reign, each to be attended by an archer, demilaunce, and a custrell, on great horses. They were so extravagantly dressed, " trapped in cloth of golde, silver, and goldsmithes woorke, and their servants richly appareled also," that " they endured not long the apparell and charges were so greate." They were not reinstated until the thirty-first year of his reign. Edward VI.'s guard was 400 strong, all very tall, and dressed in crimson velvet doublets embroidered with golden roses. In meeting Philip of Spain on his way to Winchester in 1554, Lord Arundel took 100 archers in yellow cloth striped with red velvet with their bows ready, Mary's colours, however, being white and green.

The taste for sumptuous armour became definitely fixed on the accession of Henry VIII. in 1509. Harding relates that, at the Coronation jousts, Brandon "turneyed in harneyes all over gylte from the headepeece to the Sabattons." Hall devotes scores of pages to descriptions of the magnificence of Henry, especially in presence of rival potentates or their ambassadors. Before Terouenne, the weather being very foul, Maximilian and his retinue came to the rendezvous in black cloth, but Henry was attended by a large retinue extravagantly dressed, comprising his usual "nine henxmen" in white and crimson cloth of gold richly embroidered with goldsmith's work, on great coursers as richly caparisoned, with the addition of many gold bells, and "tassels of fyne gold in bullion"—these bore his helm; "the two grangardes," his spears, axe, etc. He entered Terouenne as a conqueror in "armure gilt and graven"; and Maximilian set out on his return "toward Almaine in gilte harness, and his nobles in white harness and rich cotes." On the occasion of the French ambassador's visit to Greenwich, the king disported himself at the "tilte in a newe harnesse all gilte of a strange fashion that had not been seen." No less than 286 spears were broken. Charles V. is often represented in very richly embossed armour, and some of the suits made for him, such as by the Colmans of Augsburg, show that these sculptured and pictorial representations were not wholly imaginary.

It is not, however, until the reigns of Mary and Elizabeth that the culminating point of richness in armour is attained, when poems abound in allusions to it. In Spenser's *Faerie Queen* armour always glitters with gold, and in Camoens' *Lusiad* there are "breast-plates flaming with a thousand dyes."

Little sumptuously decorated armour was made in England, the finest that can claim to have been made here being five existing suits out of the twenty-nine in the Jacobe album. One only of these belongs to the nation, Lord Bucarte's bequeathed with the Wallace Collection; the

Fig. 23.—*Suit of late Italian Armour. Embossed and damascened. Tower of London.*

opportunity of acquiring Sir Christopher Hatton's, notwithstanding its historic interest, being hitherto neglected.

FIG. 24.—*Fine Italian Breast-plate, c. 1550. Said to have been worn by Philip of Spain. Collection of Mr. David Currie.*

Of foreign armour the suits of the Dukes of Bourbon and Montmorency at Wilton are spoils of victory, and others in the Tower and at Windsor were royal presents. The vast bulk of foreign armour in the country, however, has been acquired by purchase, and of late years. Of small collections one of the least known is that made by the grandfather of the Duke of Westminster, who purchased it from Sir Horace Walpole. The light peascod breast-plate and tassets (Fig. 22), richly

FIG. 25.—*Pair of fine Italian Gauntlets. Possibly belonging to the same Suit as the Breast-plate. Collection of Mr. David Currie.*

engraved and gilt in bands, are probably German of about 1570, and the gauntlets of approximately the same date, while the close helmet is about twenty years earlier. The finely engraved and parcel-gilt breast-plate and tassets (Plate III.) are probably Italian, dating from about 1540. A deep peascod breast-plate and tassets richly arabesqued with dolphins on a

Fig. 26.—*Embossed Gorget. French, c. 1550. Collection of Mr. David Currie.*

blue ground, bears an engraved escutcheon with the figure of a porcupine, motto and date.

One of the most sumptuously decorated suits in the Tower, for long described as that of the Black Prince, is reproduced in Fig. 23. It is

FIG. 27.—*Silver Armour of Prince Charles, afterwards Charles II. Tower of London.*

late Italian, much of it embossed with lions' heads, etc., while the plainer surfaces are entirely covered with very delicate gold ornament on russet ground. Detail of the damascening is shown in Plate IV.

Several of our illustrations are taken from Mr. David Currie's magnificent collection, part of which is deposited in the South Kensington

Museum. Very little armour is finer in its way than the breast-plate (Fig. 24) formerly in the Bernal and Londesborough collections. The repoussé work, designed in the best Italian taste of the sixteenth century, is enhanced by gold damascening on backgrounds gilt and inlaid with silver. It is said to have been worn by Philip of Spain, the steel gauntlets (Fig. 25), of similar work, having perhaps formed part of the same suit. It recalls one in Madrid presented to the Infant Philip III. by the Duke of Terranova. The finely embossed breast-plate (Plate V.), and gorget (Fig. 26), are French, but unfortunately no history attaches to them.

This extremely costly armour, with no defensive quality, was intended for parade rather than use, and an appropriate head-piece was also

FIG. 28.—*Sixteenth century Armet of rare form, with double visor.* Mr. E. Cozens Smith.

especially devised for triumphal display. This was the casque, based on classic models, which left the face entirely uncovered. Artists of high renown, like Verrocchio and Pollajuolo, designed and worked upon these *casques d'honneur*, and the Negrolis, Colmans, and other famous armourers vied with each other in their production. Superb examples exist in the great national collections of Europe, but rarely find their way into private hands. Plate VI., not one of the finest examples, was formerly in Lord Londesborough's, and now in Mr. Currie's collection. It has a triple comb and plume-holder, and is believed to have formed part of the armour of an officer of the guard to Cosmo de' Medici.

The casque passes almost insensibly into the more serviceable burgonet, a classic-looking helmet with ear-pieces and neck-covering, dear to Salvator Rosa and his contemporaries. This developed into the spider

FIG. 29.—*Suit of parcel-gilt Armour. Made for Prince Charles, afterwards Charles I. Tower of London.*

helmet with bars to protect the face, and the open and barred helmets of Charles I. and the Commonwealth. Fig. 27 represents an extremely rich example of the latter, made with cuirass and gorget in repoussé silver for

FIG. 30.—*Richly Embossed and Damascened Target. Italian, sixteenth century.*
Mr. David Currie's Collection.

Charles II. when prince. The defensive quality of the armet, not being so purely consecrated to parade, was rarely impaired by embossing, and even when made for monarchs, the decoration was mainly confined to etching and gilding. A rare form with double visor, five rope-like combs, and bands of engraving, is illustrated (Fig. 28) from the collection of Mr. Cozens Smith of Benyeo. The armet continued to be used by mounted officers until the middle of the seventeenth century, a picture of Rocroy, 1643, showing Condé in a hat, but his staff in visored helmets. One of the latest cap-à-pie suits, probably never worn, is that in the Tower, richly worked and gilded all over, presented to Charles I. by the City of London.

The high-combed morions and cabassets of the pikemen and musketeers are generally richly etched in vertical bands, or covered with interlacing arabesques, which we gather, from numerous passages in Brantôme's works, were usually gilt. Thus 4000 harquebuziers stepped out of the ranks as *enfans perdus*, at the call of Mons. d'Andelet " tous morions gravez et dorez en teste."

The buckler or target appears an archaic defence, but survived with us, sometimes in high favour like the sword, at others nearly obsolete, until the reign of James I., and in Scotland till recent times. It was banished while the Spanish rapier and left-handed dagger were in use.

The most magnificent targets were made solely for parade, and were borne in front of princely personages by their esquires. The broad surfaces they presented for decoration, and the esteem they were held in, induced even very great artists, like Giulio Romano, not only to design them, but actually to work upon them. It is far from rare to find in collections of drawings by old masters, designs for shields, like those signed Polydore and B. Franco hanging in the corridors at Chatsworth. Under the Tudor and later Valois kings they were usually round and of steel, but sometimes elliptical, obovate, vesica-shaped, rectangular, and even heater-shaped, with painted arms. One of the finest ever produced is the Milanese buckler at Windsor, believed to have been in England since the time of Francis I. The repoussé work is of most exquisite finish and the gold damascening of extraordinary delicacy. Others not inferior to it are at Dresden, Turin, and Madrid, the latter by Colman of Augsburg. The shield of Charles IX. in the Louvre is also superbly damascened. Magnificent specimens are known from the hands of the Negrolis and Picinino of Milan, Gasparo Mola of Florence, Giorgio Ghisi of Mantua. A description of one, now lost, by Hieronymus Spacini of Milan, states that it comprised forty-eight engravings in

PLATE VII.—Lower part of enriched Chanfron. Suit presented to Charles I. by the City of London. Tower of London.

gold upon niello. Hans Mielich has left several designs, some of which were carried out by Colman. The finely-embossed target in the Kensington Museum is signed by Georgius Sigman of Augsburg. The Bernal, Meyrick, Soltykoff, and other collections now dispersed, included

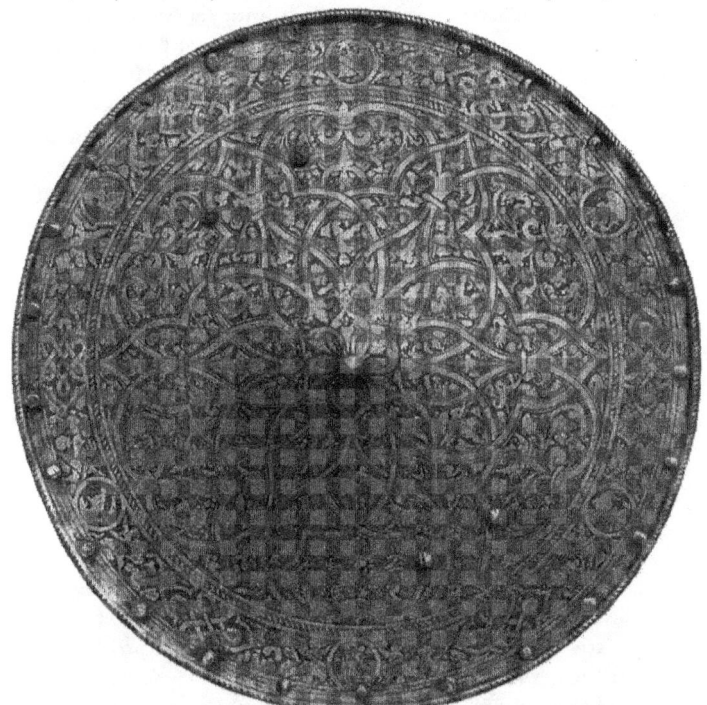

FIG. 31.—*Target of Etched Steel. Italian or German, about* 1550. *Mr. P. Davidson's Collection.*

examples illustrating the story of Coriolanus, Siege of Troy, Judgment of Paris, etc.

Those intended to receive the hard knocks of active service must have presented unembossed surfaces, though perhaps richly etched and gilded like the morions. The specimen (Fig. 30) belonging to Mr. Currie is rich enough for parade, with its bands of embossing and fine damascening, while the second illustration (Fig. 31) might have been the war target of an Italian or Spanish Captain under Philip II. It is remarkable that the first Greenwich inventory only contains eight bucklers, "of steele, seven guilte and wroughte." They were probably somewhat like Fig. 31. Another among the jewels was of silver gilt, with the arms of England, roses, castles, and pomegranates. This, like the quaint little roundel belonging to Lord Kenyon (Fig. 32), was probably English. It appears that London bucklers acquired some celebrity in the time of Elizabeth, who limited the length of their steel points to two inches, for the young King of Scots greatly desired to possess one. George Brownfelde, Roger Morgan, Tothill Street, and Richard Hamkyn, King Street, Westminster,

FIG. 32.—*Roundel with National Badges and Inscription. Belonging to Lord Kenyon.*

were buckler-makers to Henry VIII.; and Peter Lovat, a Frenchman, supplied steel pavices at the sign of the cock in Fleet Street at eight shillings each. They are seldom mentioned as playing a part in actual warfare, though when Lord Grey de Wilton called for forlorn hopes at the siege of Guynes, fifty stept out "with swordes and roondelles to view and essaye the breatches." The celebrated Jarnac duel, witnessed by Henri II., was fought with sword and target.

The chanfron or head-piece to the horse's armour, originally called the chevron, received as much attention as the helmet or buckler of its rider. It was the pride of the noble, when Monstrelet wrote, to make the horse's head-front blaze with jewels. Designs for horse-armour by Hans Mielich, and that actually executed for Christian II. at Dresden, are as rich as the suits themselves. The latter illustrates the labours of

Fig. 33.—*Hilt of Two-handed Sword with the Bear and Ragged Staff on the Pommel and Quillons in chased steel. Penshurst.*

Hercules, and is the one for which Colman received 14,000 crowns. The chanfron bears a spike, an appendage dating back to the time of Edward III. In the *Anturs of Arthur* we read—

> Opon his chèveronne be-forn
> Stode as a unicorn
> Als scharpe as a thorn,
> An nanlas of stele.

The charger ridden by Lord Scales in his tourney with the Bastard of Burgundy had a "schaffrõ with a large sharpe pyke of stele," which, penetrating the nostrils of the Bastard's steed, caused it to rear and throw him. The oldest chanfron handed down is that in Warwick Castle, which was there when visited by Sir William Dugdale. The lower part of one belonging to the suit, Fig. 29, is seen in Plate VII.

FIG. 34.—*Venetian Cinquedea, engraved, with Ivory Handle. The Duke of Norfolk.*

Swords varied considerably in the sixteenth century, the extremes sometimes meeting in the same army, the two-handed sword, scimitar, rapier, sabre, cinquedea, falchion, and malchus, being borne perhaps simultaneously by the mercenary bands comprised in it. The two-handed sword represents the largest dimensions ever attained by this weapon, perhaps originating in the sword of state, like that of Edward III. in Westminster Abbey. It was used in Scotland at an early period; if not wielded by whole clans, certainly by champions of exceptional vigour. Thus Froissart relates that Sir Archibald Douglas fought on foot and wielded an immense sword, the blade of which was two ells long, and so heavy that scarcely any other man could have lifted it from the ground. This great sword is the real claymore, though the name has been mis-appropriated to the Scottish basket-hilted broadsword of the last century. The Swiss and Germans were the only people who made it an offensive weapon for large disciplined bodies of troops, and in the sixteenth century it had become an essentially Teutonic weapon. Henry VIII.'s great personal strength and agility enabled him to wield it, as a young man, and to withstand all-comers. The fine hilt illustrated (Fig. 33)

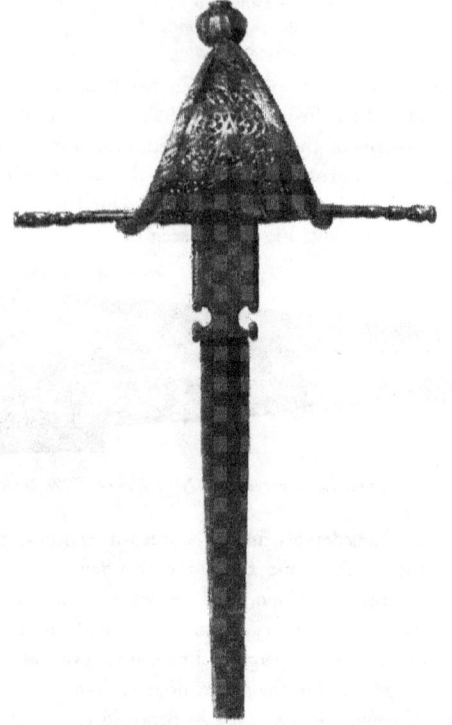

FIG. 35.—*Main-Gauche with Steel Hilt. Belonging to Mr. Percy Macquoid.*

from Penshurst, with the pommel and quillons carved and chased out of the solid steel into the bears and ragged staff of the Leicesters, is undoubtedly the most beautiful in the country. The blade has been shortened, perhaps under the edict of Queen Elizabeth, who posted guards at the City Gates to break all swords that were too long.

In striking contrast to this is the well-known Cinquedea, the Italian

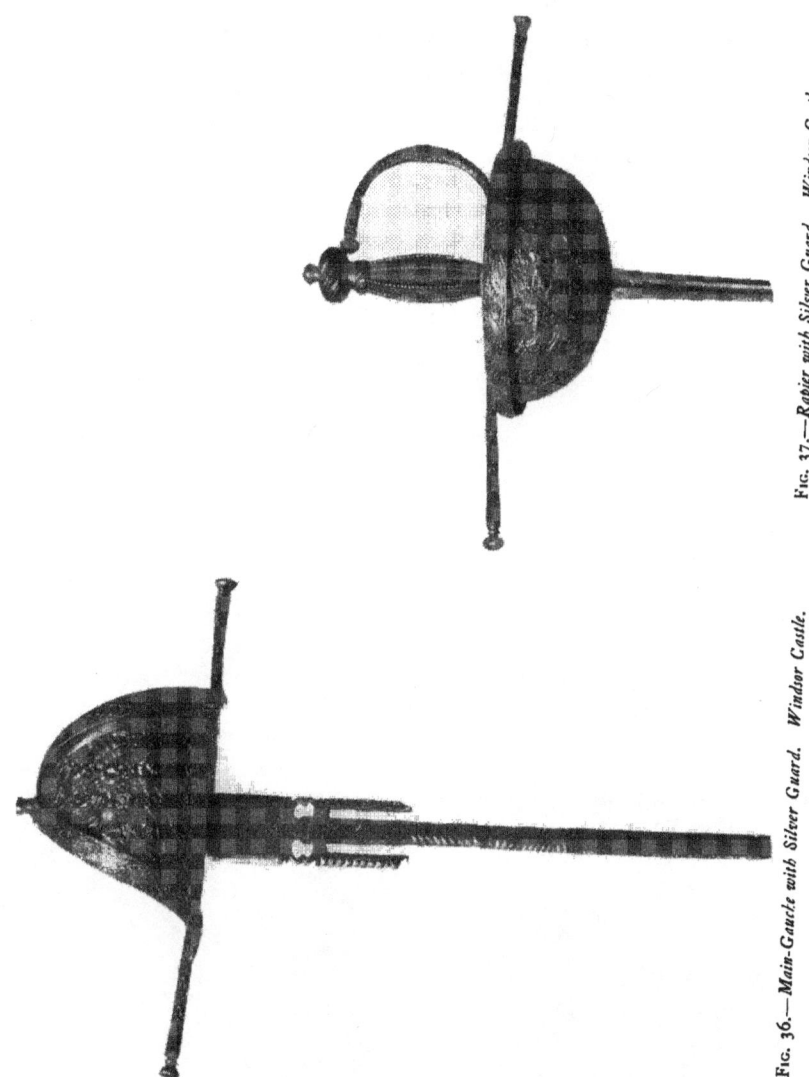

Fig. 36.—Main-Gauche with Silver Guard. Windsor Castle.

Fig. 37.—Rapier with Silver Guard. Windsor Castle.

translation of the French *Sang de dez*. The name of a spear, *langue-de-bœuf*, has been improperly applied to it since the eighteenth century. The handles were frequently ivory with pierced brass insertions, like the illustration (Fig. 34), belonging to the Duke of Norfolk; but the finest

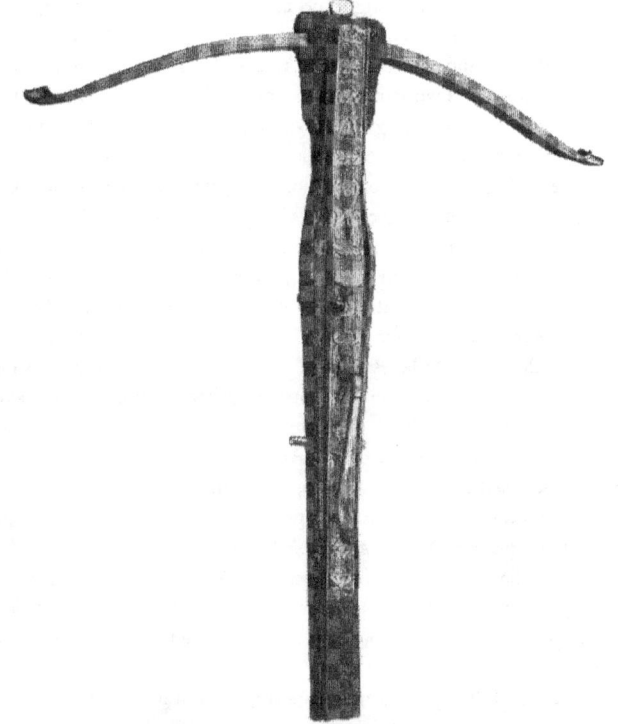

FIG. 38.—*Inlaid Ivory Cross-bow. Tower of London.*

examples are of chased steel, exquisitely worked and silvered. The Cinquedea was highly esteemed in Venice.

Until the introduction of the Spanish rapier the sword used with the buckler was short and heavy in the blade, though with handles sometimes richly worked and inlaid with silver. The rapier appeared about 1570 to 1580, the slender tapering blade being relatively of great length, rendering it difficult to sheathe. The guards to the hilts were generally of open work, the variety of form, though endless, falling into three leading groups, the swept-hilted, shell-guard, and cup-hilted, the finest workmanship being as a rule found on the latter. The quillons, generally very long, are either straight or curved. With the rapier, a long dagger held in the left hand and called the *main-gauche* was used to parry, the blade being notched near the base to entangle and break the opponent's weapon. Two varieties are figured, both with superbly chased hilts; the one of steel belonging to Mr. Percy Macquoid (Fig. 35), and one with silver guard (Fig. 36), belonging to Her Majesty. The cup-hilted rapier (Fig. 37), reproduced on a slightly smaller scale, is the companion to the latter dagger and is also partly silver-hilted and chased with representations of combats. The quillons are engraved with flowers, and the blade is signed Heinrich Coell, Solingen. The blades and hilts were frequently, perhaps usually, made in different workshops. Many of those in Vienna have German hilts and Italian blades, others have Solingen blades and Milanese hilts. Toledo blades were, however, preferred, and their marks were frequently imitated by German makers. The first ship of the ill-fated Spanish Armada to fall a prey to Drake and Howard was the *Capitana* of the Andalusian squadron, which among its treasures carried a chest of swords, richly mounted, and intended for presentation to the English Catholic peers. Frequent reference is made in Elizabethan plays to Bilbao and Toledo blades, but more especially to "Foxes," so called from the Nuremberg mark. Certain passages show that these were used with the buckler, in this country at least; and in the engraving of the funeral of Sir Philip Sidney, targets both round and oval are carried.

The staves, bills, pikes, morris-pikes, holy-water sprinklers, etc., played a very important part in war at this period. The halberds and partisans carried by officers of the harquebusiers, royal guards, and officials were the vehicles for an immense amount of decoration, especially throughout the seventeenth century. Albert Dürer, writing from Venice to Pirkheimer, mentions that the Italian lansquenets "have roncoins with 218 points, and if they pink a man with any of these, the man is dead, as they are all poisoned." This could hardly have been serious, but a sheet of drawings by Leonardo da Vinci shows some very extraordinary forms. Most of the varieties of staves were no doubt originally developments of the peasant scythes, bill-hooks, pitch-forks, and the poll-axe; each country preserving some peculiar form. The cross-bow had long ceased to be a military weapon, but was, owing to its silent fire, still in great repute for sport. It was usually inlaid with ivory, engraved, sometimes stained and heightened with pearl. A fine specimen in the Tower is illustrated (Fig. 38).

V

FIREARMS AND GUNLOCKS

By Major V. A. FARQUHARSON

The actual date of the first employment of portable firearms is uncertain, but representations of them are frequently met with in the illustrated MSS. of the early part of the fifteenth century, their form at first being simply a tube fastened to a wooden stock, and, according to the coloured drawings, the tube was either of brass or iron. The manner of firing was to apply a match by hand to a touch-hole situated on the upper part of the barrel. The first improvement was to drill the touch-hole in the side of the barrel, with the priming held in a pan formed in a projection also on the side of the barrel, which had a cover, moving on a pivot, thus protecting the powder from the wet or wind till the moment of firing, when it was pushed back by hand. This was the general kind of firearm used during the first half of the fifteenth century. For some time after their introduction, hand firearms were viewed with disfavour, and it was considered more or less unfair to employ them, seeing that the Gothic armour worn by the knights had power to resist the ordinary weapons of the field, but took no account of the effects of missiles from the clumsy "gonner." That they were in use in 1453 is evident, as the great Talbot, 1st Earl of Shrewsbury, buried at Whitchurch, came to his end from this cause. "Though at first with manfull courage and sore fighting the Earle wanne the entre of their camp, yet at length they compassed him about, and, *shooting him through the thigh with an hand-gonne,* slew his horse and finally killed him lying on the ground,

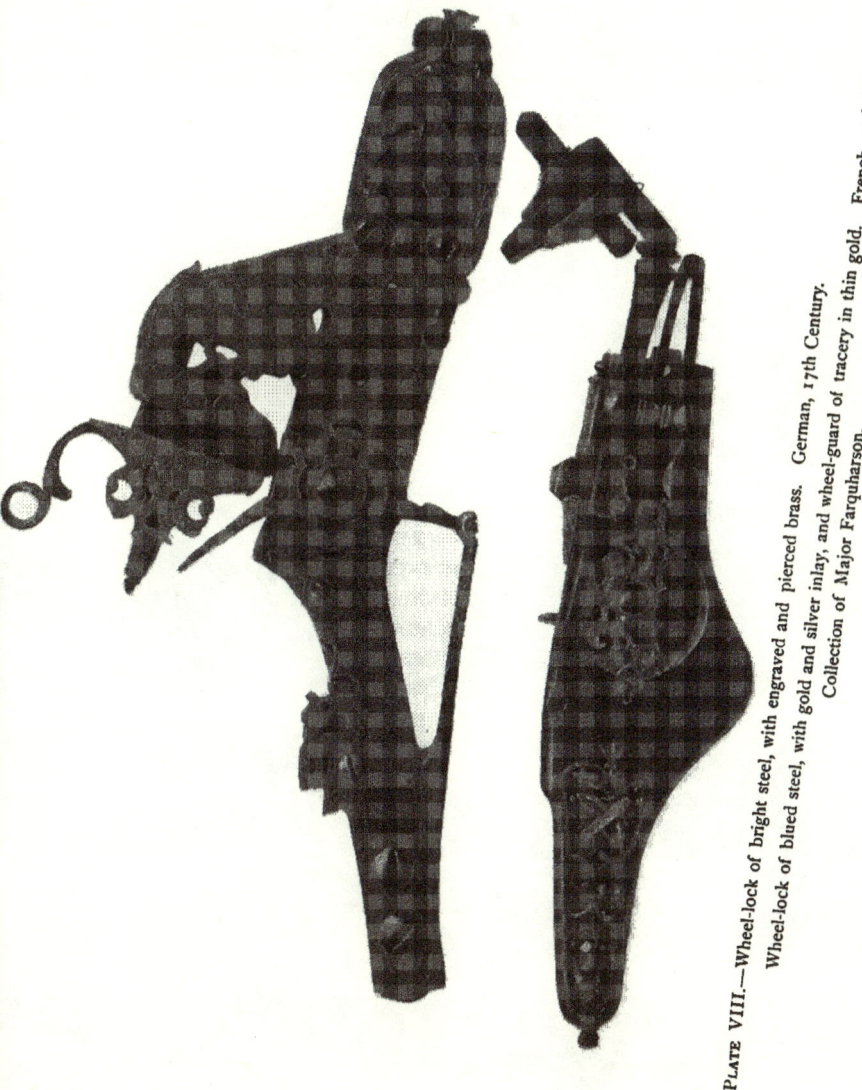

PLATE VIII.—Wheel-lock of bright steel, with engraved and pierced brass. German, 17th Century. Wheel-lock of blued steel, with gold and silver inlay, and wheel-guard of tracery in thin gold. French, 17th Century.
Collection of Major Farquharson.

whom they never durst look in the face, while he stood on his feet" (Hollinshed's *Chronicle*). This was at Chatillon, 20th July 1453.

The first lock was apparently a curved piece of metal in the shape of an S and pivoted in the centre, the upper point holding the match, the lower part, which was prolonged like the lever in the cross-bow, by its weight keeping the match from the pan till this lower part was compressed to the stock on firing.

The next stage was the matchlock proper. This is the first lock where the mechanism is complete on a plate. The cock is kept back by a spring acting on the long arm of a lever, while fastened to the short end was a sear or trigger. The pan still projects on the side of the barrel, a principle seen in modern Eastern matchlocks. The next matchlocks had the pan fixed to and forming part of the plate ; later matchlocks only vary in the shape of the plate. In the reign of William III. the plates are of the same size as the flint-lock, so that the locks could be changed when required. The matchlock was altogether in use for nearly 200 years, owing to its great simplicity and cheapness. There is a variation of the matchlock in which, by elaborate mechanism, the match is caused to descend on the priming with a snap-action. It is difficult to see the advantage to be obtained from this, as the match it would appear must have broken by contact with the pan, unless it may have taken the form of a stick of hard composition. The head of the match-holders in these locks is a short tube, which gives some probability to this theory, but there is no record to prove it.

The *wheel-lock* is supposed to have been invented in 1517, although a lock belonging to the writer has the date of 1509, yet it is not certain if 1569 is not meant. Nuremberg is reported to be the place of its invention, where indeed, at the time, most things were claimed to have been invented ; and the city mark is constantly met with on early locks. It was an important invention, and, except for the delicacy of its mechanism and great expense of production, it was an efficient lock. It consisted briefly of a steel wheel, having from two to four grooves affixed to an axle which passed through the lock-plate, the edge of the wheel appearing through the bottom of the pan. The outer part of the axle was square for a key to fit on, and the inner had a shoulder or crank, which was connected by a shackle chain of three links to an extremely strong spring. The fire stone (pyrites) was fixed in a holder, screwed to the farther end of the lock-plate. The pan had a sliding cover. To put the lock in action a key or "spanner" was placed on the outer end of the axle, and given a ¾ turn; by this the spring was compressed, and kept at tension by the nose of a sear, connected with the trigger, entering a small hole on the inner surface of the wheel. The pan was then primed, the sliding cover brought over it, and the pyrites holder depressed, bringing the pyrites down on the cover. On pulling the trigger the wheel revolved, its axle shoulder knocked back the pan cover and allowed the grooves to grate sparks from the firestone, thus firing the priming. There are numerous variations in the wheel-lock of all dates and of many nationalities. By the shape of the feeds, the number of grooves, and by the internal mechanism, and of course by the ornamentation, a tolerable idea can be got of the date or origin of a piece. It is remarkable that the earliest locks were more complete and had appliances that we fail to find in the later. Thus in Fig. 40, a type of the earliest pistol, the lock possesses a safety catch to prevent premature discharge, also a spring-catch to keep the pan cover back. Those, which would be thought advantages, are not to be found in the two examples in Plate VIII. of later date and finer workmanship. In some cases the wheel winds itself, when the pyrites holder is drawn back, thus dispensing with a key. This principle is such an obvious improvement that it seems strange it was not universally adopted.

A result of the introduction of the wheel-lock was the invention of pistols, which never carry match-locks. The name may have been derived from Pistoia in Tuscany, or, as it has been suggested, from the name of the coin pistole, referring to the bore. There is a word in Italian *pistolese*, but it signifies a knife. Fig. 40 is a good example of an early pistol. It is of the class used by the Reiters, German cavalry, the first body of troops armed with pistols. The barrels at this time are of great thickness, owing to the dread of bursting, and the stocks sloped abruptly, being terminated by a ball butt. This was probably to act as a counterpoise, and also to facilitate drawing the piece from the holster. It would be more efficient, too, when used as a club, as it very frequently was, according to pictures of the time. In

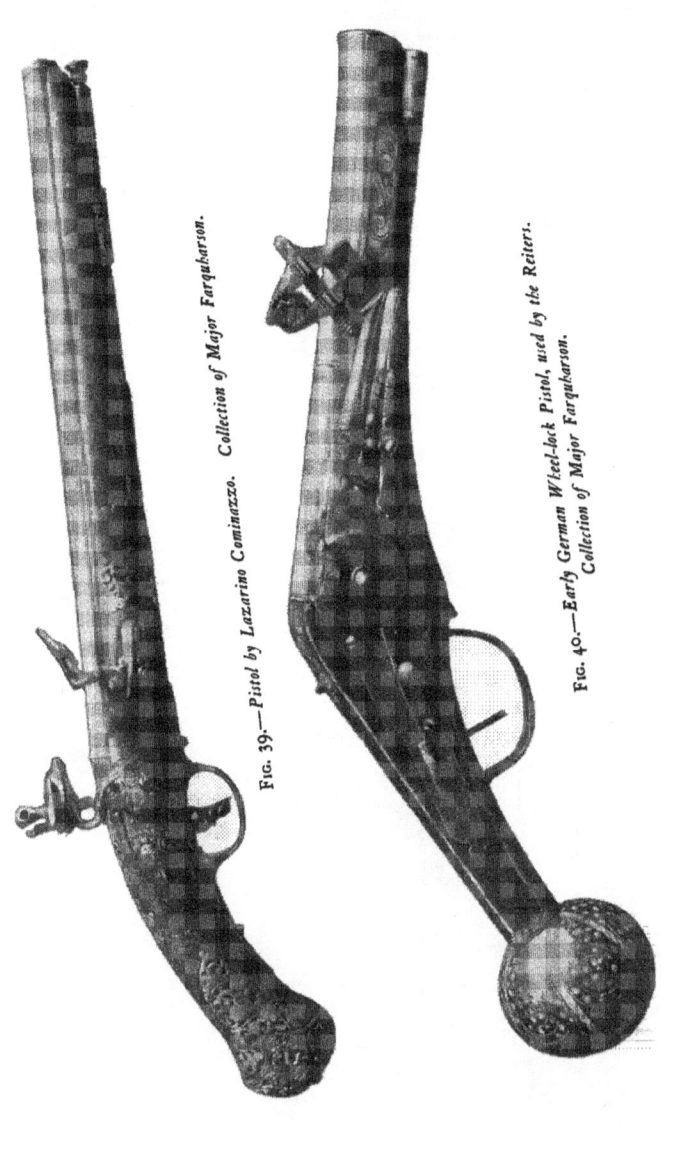

Fig. 39.—*Pistol by Lazarino Cominazzo. Collection of Major Farquharson.*

Fig. 40.—*Early German Wheel-lock Pistol, used by the Reiters. Collection of Major Farquharson.*

early engravings of the Reiter he is armed not only with a pair, but on occasion with four of these pistols, two in the holsters and two fastened to his belt by hasps (Fig. 40 is furnished with a hook or hasp on the reverse side). The Reiter also had a sword. The introduction of the pistol altered the tactics of war ; the bodies of horse no longer charged home, but galloped up by ranks, within a few paces of the enemy, discharged their pistols, and then wheeled outward by half troops towards each flank, leaving the front clear for the succeeding rank to take their place. They then reloaded and re-formed ready for another advance. Many of the earlier pistols were wholly of steel. The smaller pistols had a flat butt, cut slanting, and were called Dags. In course of time the barrels were made longer and thinner, the stocks became more straight, and the ball butt elongated, and finally disappeared. The wheel-lock was used for pistols up to 1650. Crusoe, in the Instructions for the Cavallerie, 1632, gives some fifteen motions for the "firing Exercise" of the wheel pistol.

The Queen possesses a double-barrelled wheel rifle, in which one barrel was placed vertically over the other, dated 1588. It is fired by means of two wheel-locks on one plate, in one of which the works are outside, and the other has them hidden by the plate, the stock is of dark wood, and the fittings of the locks are of chased and gilt metal. Its double barrel, date of the rifling, and the fact of its having a steel ramrod, all make it remarkable. The Dresden arms are on the heel plate, a cypher HF on the stock, and the barrel has a bear as armourer's mark.

The wheel-lock was rarely used for infantry arms, but was of necessity employed by cavalry, where the match was inconvenient.

The next form of lock was the *Snap-hance*, evolved from the wheel-lock by converting the pyrites holder into a fire-steel, and replacing the wheel by a hammer, acted on by a spring and affixed to the opposite side of the pan. The pan and cover remained the same, and the latter slid back as the hammer fell on the steel, leaving the powder bare for the sparks to fall on.

The earliest actual lock of this sort is on a pair of pistols in the Dresden Armoury, dated 1598. The pistols are of the Scotch form, but are probably of Spanish make, as the Highlanders obtained their firearms largely from Spain.

The example Fig. 42 is a snap-hance of Italian make, but of later type (about 1640). It was selected on account of the beautiful chiselled steel of which it is composed. This is in three degrees of relief. The hammer has two dragons entwined on it, and the plate and fire-steel are very richly fashioned, having the armourer's signature on it, GIOVANNI · VATE · BORGOGNONE · IN · BRESCIA. Part of the fire-steel is missing.

The most famous makers of firearms of the middle of the seventeenth century lived in Brescia, such as Lazarino Cominazzo, father and son, Lazaro Lazarino, Francino, and others. Their weapons were famed for extreme lightness and beauty of decoration.

Fig. 39 is a late example of Cominazzo's work. The barrel has a beautiful fluted twist on it, and the lock-plate and hammer, as well as the butt, are chiselled in high relief. These armourers made weapons with each class of lock. It was quite the thing for any one on their grand tour to visit Brescia, and bring back one of these famed weapons. Evelyn in his *Diary* tells us how he paid a visit to "old Lazarino Cominazzo," and got from him a carbine for which he paid a good deal of money. He seems to have been rather proud of his acquisition, as he more than once alludes to it.

The Civil War in England showed firearms in use with all four classes of lock. The infantry on both sides were chiefly armed with the heavy musket fired from a rest, having the match-lock. The cavalry had carbines fitted with snap-hances or the early complete flint, or were provided with wheel-locks.

The wheel-lock disappears from military arms about 1670, but continued in use in Germany for sporting rifles until a much later date. The *Flint-lock* proper came into use about 1630. The earliest specimens appear to be Spanish. The mainspring in these was on the outside of the lock-plate, and the mechanism of the simplest character, consisting of a catch forming a ledge, protruding to the outside of the lock-plate, for the foot of the hammer to rest on when cocked, and on this ledge being drawn back on pressing the trigger the hammer falls, striking the steel, which also covers the pan.

The example Fig. 43 is one of a class where the ornamentation is very elaborate. The design is formed mostly by the chisel and hammer, and even in the internal mechanism the file appears scarcely to have been

Fig. 41.—*Richly Decorated Flint-lock. Probably Spanish.
Collection of Major Farquharson.*

Fig. 42.—*Snap-hance of Italian make, about 1640.
Collection of Major Farquharson.*

used. Many of these fine locks exist, but never have any armourer's mark on them; the mechanism, however, points to their Spanish origin. Works of this description were found in Spanish locks to the latter end of the eighteenth century. In both English and French flint-locks the mechanism was on the inside of the lock-plate, and a tumbler connected the hammer with the action of the mainspring. A later improvement was to add a bridle to give two bearings for the tumbler axle, and a small swivel connecting the tumbler with the mainspring, both of these improvements ensuring greater smoothness in the action. This form of improved mechanism was continued in the percussion lock,

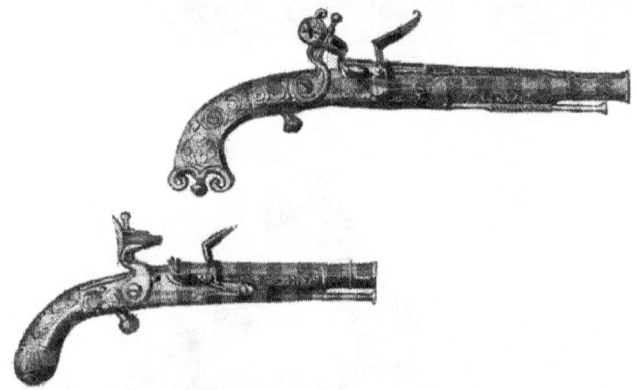

FIGS. 43, 44.—*Highland Pistols. Collection of Major Farquharson.*

after the use of a flint was discontinued, and, indeed, the hammer used in the first military breechloader generally employed in our army, the Snider, was acted on by mechanism of much the same sort.

Figs. 43 and 44 show specimens of the Highland pistol, a class which stands quite by itself. These weapons no doubt were evolved from the early steel wheel dags in common use in Germany. Many Highlanders were to be found in the armies of other European nations, whence they probably took the fashion and also procured their firearms. The earliest weapons of the sort, as well as the latest, were all of steel (or rarely brass). The stocks had a heart-shaped butt, and were furnished with snap-hance locks. There is one of this description, undoubtedly a Scotch weapon, in the armoury in the old castle of Nürnberg, where the arms have always been stored, belonging probably to one of the many Scotch officers employed in Germany during the wars of the seventeenth century. Later on the butt of the pistol assumed a claw form and the ordinary flint-lock was employed, the mechanism, however, being of a distinctive sort, possibly of Dutch origin. The latest of these pistols have a rounded butt as in Fig. 44. The ornament found on the back of the hammer in Fig. 43 is not to be seen in any other class of lock.

The Highlanders looking at length on their weapons as part of the equipment of their national garb, a colony of armourers sprang up in the village of Doune in Stirlingshire, a place where "trysts" or fairs were held, and where the Highlanders resorted to exchange their cattle for other goods. The following account is given in *Scottish National Memorials*, of this trade of Doune. "The only remains of any of the ancient branches of trade is the making of Highland pistols. The reputation of Doune for this manufacture, about the time of the German war, was very great. This art was introduced to Doune about the year 1646 by Thomas Caddell, who having been instructed in his craft at Muthil, a village in Strathearn in Perthshire, came and settled at Doune. This famous tradesman possessed a most profound genius, and an inquisitive mind, and though a man of no education and remote from every means of instruction in the mechanical arts, his study and persevering exertions brought his art to so high a degree of perfection that no pistols made in Britain excelled or perhaps equalled those of his making either for sureness, strength, or beauty. He taught the trade to his children and several apprentices, of whom was one John Campbell, whose son and grandson carried on the business. While the ancient dress of Caledonia was worn, that is, the 'philabeg' belted-plaid, pistols, and dirk, the pistols made in Doune excelled all others, and acquired superior reputation over France and Germany; a pair superbly ornamented were fabricated by a tradesman taught in Doune, and by the city of Glasgow given in compliment to the Marquis de Bouillé. The above Mr. Campbell's grandson, who has now given over business, made pistols for the first nobility in Europe, as Prince Ferdinand of Brunswick, the Hereditary Prince of Brunswick, the Duke of Cumberland, and others. The trade is now (1798) carried on by John Murdoch (the maker of Fig. 44). These pistols were sold (1798) at from four to twenty-four guineas a pair."

The names of some of these armourers were the Caddells, James Sutherland, Thomas Murdoch, John Murdoch, S. Michie, John Campbell, J. Stuart, David M'Kenzie, and others. The trade died out at the commencement of this century.

These weapons were remarkable for grace of outline and great lightness. The butt has a small knob, which, when unscrewed, forms a picker to clear the touch-hole with. The mainsprings in many cases appear to be weak, having little room to work in the slender stocks.

INDEX

Almayne rivets, 14, 15
Ambras Collection, 48
Archers, 36-38, 52, 56, 60
Armet, 32, 36, 44, 48, 51, 53, 71, 72
Arthur, King, 8, 12, 21
Arundel, Lord, 60
Arundel Society, 40
Augsburg, 40, 41, 60

Back-plates, 28, 29, 40, 44
Bastard of Burgundy, 77
Battle Abbey, Arms of, 53
Bavier, The, 53
Bayeux Tapestry, 18
Beauchamp, Effigy of, 24, 30
Bedford, Duke of, 38
Bernabo Visconti (Statue of), 20
Bernal Collection, 14, 68, 73
Black Prince, 10
Böheim, 40, 41
Bohun, Sir Humphrey de, 14
Bourbon, Duke of, 11, 63
Bourdonasses, 36, 37
Bows and Arrows, 38
Brantôme, 14-16, 72
Brassey, Mr. Leonard, 11
Breast-plates, 15, 28-30, 37, 40, 44, 47, 60, 64, 68
Brescia, 15, 90
  Battle before, 36
Brett Collection, 12
British Museum, 10, 17, 47, 53
Brittany, Duke of, 14
Brooke, Lord, 11
Bucarte, Lord, 60
Burges Collection, 10, 19, 47
Burgundian Armour, 49-51
Burgundy, Duke of, 14, 38

Cabassets, 72
Cadell, Thomas (Armourer), 93-94
Cajazzo, Count, 40
Calais, 38
Canterbury, 54
Cap-à-pie Armour, 6, 7, 11, 23, 27, 29, 32, 44, 46, 51, 56, 72
Capitana, The, Capture of, 82
Cassel, Battle of, 8
Chain Mail, *see* Mail Armour

Charles I., 71, 72
Charles V., 16, 60
Charolois, Count of, 53
Chatsworth, 72
Chausses, 18
Christian II., 74
Cinquedea, The, 81
Civil War in England, 90
Cœur-de-Lion, 17
Colman Family (Armourers), 40, 60, 68, 72
Colman, Lorenz, 28, 41
Cologne, 12, 13
Cominazzo (Maker of Firearms), 90
Commines, Philip de, 32, 36, 38, 53
Constantinople, 25
Corselets, 14, 48
Cosimo, Piero di, 47
Cosson, Baron de, 54
Coutts-Lindsay Collection, 12
Crests, 32, 48, 53
Crossbows, 15, 83
Crossbow-men, 36
Cuirasses, 14, 71
Cumberland, Earl of, 11
Currie, Mr. David, 12, 67, 68, 73

Damascened Armour, 22, 67, 68
Dillon, Lord, 9
Douglas, Sir Archibald, 77
Doune (Stirlingshire), 93
Dover Castle Collection, 10
Doyac, John, 14
Dugdale, Sir William, 77
Dukes of Albany and Orleans, Fight between, 38

Ear-pieces, 68
Edward I., 22
Edward III., 77
Edward VI., 10, 38, 60
Elbow-guards, 30

Farleigh Castle, 11
Flint-locks, 90
Flodden, Battle of, 7
Florence, 15
Fluted Armour, 11, 41, 43, 44, 47, 51, 53
Fornovo, Battle of, 36

Frederick the Victorious, 39
French Revolution (Destruction of Armour), 24, 25
Froissart, 16, 17

Gage, Sir John, 53
Galatin, 17
Gauntlets, 42, 44, 64, 68
Ghisi, Giorgio, 72
Gilded Armour, 60
Gordon, Mr. Panmure, 46
Gorget, The, 71
Greenwich, 9
Grünewalt, Hans (Armourer), 40
Grünewalt, Heinrich, 40
Guidarelli, Guidarello (Effigy of), 36

Halberds, 39
Hall, 24, 38, 52, 60
Harding, 60
Harold, 18
Hatton, Sir Christopher, 63
Hauberk, The, 18, 19
Head-pieces, 51, 53, 60
Helm, 39, 43, 51, 60
Helmets, 18, 20, 28, 32, 41, 48, 68, 71, 72
  Tilting, 51, 52
Henry IV., 8, 14, 54
Henry V., 8
Henry VI., 60
Henry VII., 16, 38, 51, 53, 59
Henry VIII., 9, 10, 13-15, 24, 48, 51, 52, 54, 59, 78
Herbert, Lord Richard, 37
Horse-armour, 41, 44, 46, 51, 74
Hothfield, Lord, 11
Hutin, Louis, 14, 16

Italian Armourers, 14

Jarnac and La Chateigneraye (Duel between), 22
Joan of Arc, 54
John of Eltham, 8

Kenyon, Lord, 74
Kirkener, Erasmus, 53

INDEX

Lances, 36, 37
Layard, 17
Lodelowe, Abbot Thomas de, 53
Londesborough Collection, 11, 68
Longfield, Mr. F. H., 18
Louis X., 16
Louis XI. 14, 16, 39

Macquoid, Mr. Percy, 45, 82
Madrid Armoury, 16
Mail Armour, 17, 18, 22
Mantua, Court of, 41
— Marquis of, 36
Marignan, Battle of, 14
Matchlocks, 85
Matthew of Paris, 14
Maximilian Armour, 51
Maximilian, Emperor, 9, 13, 20, 24, 40, 41, 53, 60
Medici, Cosmo de', 68
Meyrick Collection, 11, 20, 53, 73
Middle Temple Hall, 18
Mielich, Hans, 73, 74
Milan, 13, 14, 39
Milan, Duke of, 14
Milanese Armour, 14, 40
— Buckler, 72
Missaglias, The (Armourers), 39, 40
Mola, Gasparo, 72
Monstrelet, 14, 17
Montfort, Simon de, 22
Montlhéry, Battle of, 38, 53
Montmorency, Duke of, 11, 63
Moorish Steel-Workers, 15, 16
Morion, 16, 72

National Gallery, 20, 21, 30, 32, 47
Neck-guards, 68
Negrolis, The (Armourers), 68
Netherlandish Armour, 16
Nineveh, 17, 20
Norfolk, Duke of, 13, 81
Nucius, Nicander, 59
Nuremberg, 28, 40, 44, 45, 85

Otterbourne, Battle of, 12
Otto IV., Count, Figure of, 30
Oxford, Earl of, 37

Paton, Sir Noël, 12, 19, 22, 26, 28, 53
Pauldron, The, 40, 44
Pearson, Sir Wheatman, 11, 46
Pembroke, Earl of, 11
Penshurst Castle Collection, 11, 52, 78
Perugino, 30
Philip II., 74
Picinino (Milan), 72
Pistols, 86, 92
Plate Armour, 23
Plumpton Correspondence, 37
Pollajuolo, 68
Pommel, The, 55, 78
Pourpoint, The, 15
Pratt (Dealer in Armour), 25, 28
Prussia, King of, 46

Rapier, The, 81
Reiters (German Cavalry), 86-89
Richard II., 13
Richard III., 37
Rifles, 89
Romano, Giulio, 72
Rosa, Salvator, 68
Rosebecque, Battle of, 16
Roundel, The, 74

St. George (Figure of), 31, 32, 40
St. Michael (in full Armour), 30
St. Quentin, Battle of, 11
St. William (in Garofalo's *Madonna and Child*), 32
Sant' Egidio, Battle of, 32
Sallads, 14, 24, 25, 29, 40, 52, 53
Saxony, Duke of, 43
Scales, Lord, 77
Shoulder-guards, 30, 36, 51
Shrewsbury Collection, 12
Sidney, Sir Philip, 52, 82
Sigman, Georgius, 73
Smith, Mr. Cozens, 72
Smith, Sir James, 56
Snap-hance Lock, 89, 90
Sollerets, 28, 29, 30, 32, 39, 40, 52, 53
Soltykoff Collection, 73
South Kensington Museum, 10, 30, 35, 36
Spacini, Hieronymus, 72

Spain, Philip of, 17
Spanish Armada, 82
Spurs, Battle of the, 19
Stafford, Lord, 44
Standard Collar of Mail, 21, 22
Strozzi, 14
Suffolk, Duke of, 52, 60
Sullivan, Mr. J. F., 56
Swords, 9, 12, 15, 16, 31, 53, 54, 55, 59, 77, 82

Talbot, 1st Earl of Shrewsbury, 85
Talbot, Sir Gilbert, 16
Target, The, 72, 73, 74, 84
Tassets, 64
Terouenne, 60
Towcester, Battle of, 37
Tower, The, 9, 10, 11, 14, 44, 46, 48, 53, 63, 67, 77, 83
Tuilles, 40, 42

Uccello, Paolo, 32, 52

Verrocchio, 68
Vikings, The, 17, 18
Vinsauf, Geoffrey de 17
Vischer, Peter, 30
Visor, The, 44, 48, 51, 52, 71

Wace, 18
Wallace Collection, 10, 29, 46, 48, 53, 60
Walpole, Horace, 11, 64
Wars of the Roses, 24, 37
Warwick Castle, 77
Warwick, Earl of, 8, 9, 37, 54
Weinsberg, Count, Effigy of, 30
Westminster, 9, 10, 51, 54, 77
Westminster, Duke of, 47, 64
Wheel-lock, 85, 86
William III., 85
William of Toulouse, 8
Williams, Mr. Morgan, 41
Wilton House, 11
Wilton, Lord Grey de, 8, 9
Windsor Collection, 10, 54, 63, 82
Wolsey, 15
Woolwich Collection, 10, 20, 48
Wyatt, Costume worn by, 21

Zouche, Lord, 12, 25

THE END

Printed by R. & R. CLARK, LIMITED, *Edinburgh*

www.ingramcontent.com/pod-product-compliance
Lightning Source LLC
Chambersburg PA
CBHW021827230426
43669CB00008B/890